Institute of Leadership
& Management

# **super**series

## Understanding Change in the Workplace

### FIFTH EDITION

Published for the
Institute of Leadership & Management

ELSEVIER

AMSTERDAM • BOSTON • HEIDELBERG • LONDON • NEW YORK • OXFORD
PARIS • SAN DIEGO • SAN FRANCISCO • SINGAPORE • SYDNEY • TOKYO

Pergamon Flexible Learning is an imprint of Elsevier

Pergamon
*Flexible*
Learning

Pergamon Flexible Learning is an imprint of Elsevier
Linacre House, Jordan Hill, Oxford OX2 8DP, UK
30 Corporate Drive, Suite 400, Burlington, MA 01803, USA

First edition 1986
Second edition 1991
Third edition 1997
Fourth edition 2003
Fifth edition 2007

Editor: David Pardey

Based on material in previous editions of this work

**British Library Cataloguing in Publication Data**
A catalogue record for this book is available from the British Library

**Library of Congress Cataloguing in Publication Data**
A catalogue record for this book is available from the Library of Congress

ISBN 978-0-08-046424-4

For information on all Pergamon Flexible Learning publications
visit our website at http://books.elsevier.com

Institute of Leadership & Management
Registered Office
1 Giltspur Street
London
EC1A 9DD
Telephone: 020 7294 2470
www.i-l-m.com
ILM is part of the City & Guilds Group

Typeset by Charon Tec Ltd (A Macmillan Company), Chennai, India
www.charontec.com
Printed and bound in Great Britain

07 08 09 10 11    10 9 8 7 6 5 4 3 2 1

# ⬤ Contents

*Series preface*                                                           v
*Unit specification*                                                      vii


# Workbook introduction                                                   ix

  1   ILM Super Series study links                                        ix
  2   Links to ILM qualifications                                         ix
  3   Links to S/NVQs in management                                       ix
  4   Workbook objectives                                                  x
  5   Activity planner                                                    xi


# Session A   Creating a positive response to change                      1

  1   Introduction                                                         1
  2   Establishing a culture receptive to innovation and change            2
  3   Acknowledging resistance to change in others                         6
  4   Managing resistance to change                                       11
  5   Summary                                                             22


# Session B   Planning change                                            23

  1   Introduction                                                        23
  2   Reasons for major change                                            24
  3   Change and the first line manager                                   26
  4   Preparing for change                                                34
  5   Planning the project activities                                     40
  6   Establishing responsibilities and methods of communication          50
  7   Summary                                                             55

**Contents**

## Session C    Implementing change and managing its consequences    57

| | | |
|---|---|---|
| 1 | Introduction | 57 |
| 2 | Monitoring the project plan | 58 |
| 3 | Completing a change project | 63 |
| 4 | Summary | 69 |

## Performance checks    71

| | | |
|---|---|---|
| 1 | Quick quiz | 71 |
| 2 | Workbook assessment | 72 |
| 3 | Work-based assignment | 73 |

## Reflect and review    75

| | | |
|---|---|---|
| 1 | Reflect and review | 75 |
| 2 | Action plan | 78 |
| 3 | Extensions | 80 |
| 4 | Answers to activities | 81 |
| 5 | Answers to self-assessment questions | 81 |
| 6 | Answers to the quick quiz | 84 |
| 7 | Certificate | 85 |

# Series preface

Whether you are a tutor/trainer or studying management development to further your career, Super Series provides an exciting and flexible resource to help you to achieve your goals. The fifth edition is completely new and up-to-date, and has been structured to perfectly match the Institute of Leadership & Management (ILM)'s new unit-based qualifications for first line managers. It also harmonizes with the 2004 national occupational standards in management and leadership, providing an invaluable resource for S/NVQs at Level 3 in Management.

Super Series is equally valuable for anyone tutoring or studying any management programmes at this level, whether leading to a qualification or not. Individual workbooks also support short programmes, which may be recognized by ILM as Endorsed or Development Awards, or provide the ideal way to undertake CPD activities.

For learners, coping with all the pressures of today's world, Super Series offers you the flexibility to study at your own pace to fit around your professional and other commitments. You don't need a PC or to attend classes at a specific time – choose when and where to study to suit yourself! And you will always have the complete workbook as a quick reference just when you need it.

For tutors/trainers, Super Series provides an invaluable guide to what needs to be covered, and in what depth. It also allows learners who miss occasional sessions to 'catch up' by dipping into the series.

Super Series provides unrivalled support for all those involved in first line management and supervision.

# Unit specification

| Title: | Understanding change in the workplace | Unit Ref: | M3.02 |
|---|---|---|---|
| **Level:** | 3 | | |
| **Credit value:** | 2 | | |

| Learning outcomes<br><br>*The learner* will | Assessment criteria<br><br>*The learner* can *(in an organization with which the learner is familiar)* | |
|---|---|---|
| 1. Understand change in an organization | 1.1<br><br>1.2<br><br><br>1.3 | Explain the benefits of innovation and change for the organization<br>Identify the barriers to change and innovation in the workplace and explain practical ways of overcoming these barriers<br>Explain why communication is important in successful implementation of change |
| 2. Understand the effects of change on people and finance in an organization | 2.1 | Explain possible human and financial effects of change upon people, departments and the organization |

# Workbook introduction

## 1 ILM Super Series study links

This workbook addresses the issues of *Understanding Change in the Workplace*. Should you wish to extend your study to other Super Series workbooks covering related or different subject areas, you will find a comprehensive list at the back of this book.

## 2 Links to ILM qualifications

This workbook relates to the learning outcomes of Unit M3.02 Understanding change in the workplace from the ILM Level 3 Award, Certificate and Diploma in First Line Management.

## 3 Links to S/NVQs in management

This workbook relates to the following Unit of the Management Standards which are used in S/NVQs in Management, as well as a range of other S/NVQs:

C6. Implement change

# 4 Workbook objectives

Today change goes on all around us, all the time. It may once have been enough for a manager to fit into whatever job he or she was given and just keep things ticking along smoothly in much the same way as they always had.

Today, however, no manager can afford to accept the status quo. If an organization is to stay competitive and prosper, it must constantly change – which means that an essential part of your role as an effective manager is to initiate, plan and implement change.

As a first line manager, the type of change you implement will probably be small-scale, perhaps as part of a gradual, ongoing programme of continuous improvement, in which frequent minor changes are made to processes and products or services. In a small organization, you may also have the opportunity to implement a larger, more dramatic change that crosses departmental boundaries. But the more likely scenario is that large-scale change projects will be initiated by senior management, often in response to opportunities and threats presented by external forces. Either way, you, as a manager will need to take a major role in:

■ identifying barriers to change and ways of overcoming them;
■ planning how a change is to be implemented;
■ monitoring and evaluating what is achieved by the change;
■ dealing with the consequences of change.

In this workbook we will begin by looking at the problems you may face in bringing about change and some of the techniques you can use to overcome them. We will also examine some of the basic tools used by project planners, such as critical path diagrams and Gantt charts, and the part they play in the successful implementation and monitoring of change.

Finally, throughout the book we will be considering some of the knock-on effects and consequences of change. As you may know from your own experience, these are not always beneficial. We will look at some of the negative effects as well as the many positive ones.

## 4.1 Objectives

When you have completed this workbook you will be better able to:

■ anticipate and recognize reactions to a proposed change and overcome resistance to the change;

- plan change projects;
- manage the implementation of change;
- monitor and evaluate change projects.

# 5 Activity planner

The following Activities require some planning so you may want to look at these now.

Activity 10 asks you to review a significant change in which you and your team have been involved.

Activities 16a, 17, 18, 19, 30 and 34 ask you to consider various aspects of a past significant change project. Activities 16b, 21, 23, 24, 28 and 29 ask you to consider various aspects of a forthcoming significant change project. It would be helpful to start thinking as soon as possible about which change projects these should be.

Some or all of these Activities may provide the basis of evidence for your S/NVQ portfolio. All portfolio activities and the Work-based assignment are posted with this icon.

The icon states the elements to which the portfolio activities and Work-based assignment relate.

The Work-based Assignment on page 73 suggests that you plan a forthcoming major change in some detail, preferably with the involvement of your team. The suggestion is that you return to the change identified in Activity 18b (and on which you do further work in subsequent Activities). You might, however, wish to consider another change project, in which case it will be helpful to start thinking about what this project will be.

# Session A
# Creating a positive response to change

## 1 Introduction

Change is an inevitable part of development, and it often brings hope and opportunity.

Would you agree with the following?

■ Change can bring **new interest** to the job.
  Almost all jobs can become tedious or uninteresting after a time. A change can have the effect of re-awakening enthusiasm and of stimulating a fresh appetite for the task.

■ Change can open up new prospects for **career development.**
  Trying to make progress in your chosen career can sometimes feel the way the sailor feels, when trapped inshore in shallow water. No matter how much you desire to move on, there's nothing you can do about it – until the tide changes.

■ Change can show a **new slant on things.**
  Doing the same job, in the same team, in the same way will make you start to believe there's no other way of doing it. It isn't until you break old habits that you see there are sides to the work you haven't thought of. Change will provoke discussion, raise new questions, give new food for thought.

■ Change can provide the opportunity to learn **new skills.**
  New technology, new systems, new people – these may all bring with them the prospect of adding new strings to your bow.

■ Change can be a **challenge.**
Instituting change is a new adventure. You are a pioneer, an explorer of the unknown. Can you stay cool in the face of fire?

■ Change can provide an opportunity to **empower** the team: to give team members the scope and resources to gain more control over the work they do.

If you're concerned about motivation, the problem could be that your team members don't feel involved enough in their assigned tasks. When change occurs, it could be the right time to loosen the reins a little – or a lot.

To summarize, work is more rewarding for those who learn to identify the positive aspects of change.

Once you yourself are convinced of the positive aspects of change, you will be in a far better position to help create a culture in which everyone recognizes the benefits of change on a continuous basis.

# 2 Establishing a culture receptive to innovation and change

Managers cannot create an organizational quality culture in which people are ready to be innovative and adapt to change on their own – it has to be something that all managers, at all levels, throughout an organization are keen to be involved in. This doesn't mean that you shouldn't attempt to create a culture receptive to innovation and change within your own team, whatever the attitude of others in the organization. However, it will certainly be a lot easier for you to do this in some organizations than in others.

## Activity 1

5 mins

The table below consists of pairs of statements describing two very different types of organization. For each pair, give your organization a mark of between 1 and 5 according to where you think it lies on the scale between the two types. For example, if you think your organization is one in which all decisions are made at the top, give it a score of 1. If, however, you think it's an organization in which people at all levels have some responsibility for making decisions, give it a score of 5. Another possibility is that your organization may have handed down some responsibility for decisions, but – in your opinion – not enough, in which case you may give it a score of 3.

| Organization A | Scale | Organization B |
|---|---|---|
| There is a high level of conflict within and between teams rather than mutual trust | 1 2 3 4 5 | Relations within, and between, teams are generally friendly and based on mutual trust |
| Managers work mostly behind closed doors and dislike being interrupted | 1 2 3 4 5 | Managers are generally considerate and supportive |
| All decisions are made at the top | 1 2 3 4 5 | Decisions are made at all levels |
| Everyone's job is precisely defined | 1 2 3 4 5 | People can change their work role in ways not defined in their job descriptions |
| All training follows a fixed programme | 1 2 3 4 5 | Training is given whenever the need for new skills is identified |
| All communications pass up and down through each level | 1 2 3 4 5 | Communications run across as well as up and down |
| Communications generally take the form of one-way commands | 1 2 3 4 5 | Communications are more like two-way consultations than one-way commands |
| People receive inadequate information about what is going on within the organization | 1 2 3 4 5 | People are kept well-informed about what is going on within the organization |
| Procedures are written in stone | 1 2 3 4 5 | Suggestions for improvements to procedures are encouraged |
| People are expected to lead projects on the basis of orders from above | 1 2 3 4 5 | People are encouraged to guide projects in the way they believe they will work |

How did your organization score? If it scored between 40 and 50 points, you work in an organization where the staff are more ready to welcome innovation and change. If the score was at the lower end of the scale – under 15 points – your organization has a long way to go in creating a culture receptive to innovation and change.

As a first line manager, you can do little to change the culture of your organization on your own, but you can make some progress in developing in your own team, a culture that is receptive to change.

# Activity 2 · 5 mins

Is the culture of your team one that encourages positive attitudes to innovation and change? If not, the way in which you run your team may be the reason. To find out, tick the statements that best reflect your views. You can tick as many or as few as you want, but make sure you answer as honestly as possible.

I run my team based on the following beliefs:

a People only work hard when they have to – they need to be goaded into action. ☐

b People work hard when they feel they are working for their own benefit and what they do is meaningful to them. ☐

c It is important for the team that I am in control of everything that goes on. ☐

d It is best that all communications pass through formal channels; otherwise, there is chaos. ☐

e Everyone should be as fully informed as possible, because the most effective working relationships are based on a common understanding of needs. ☐

f Collaboration and informality work better than formality and with-holding information. ☐

g Efficiency depends on everyone having a clearly defined job to do; that way everyone knows what is expected and the work is more easily controlled. ☐

h Efficiency depends on flexible arrangements, so that workteams can adapt to changing requirements more easily. People should be able to move freely from activity to activity, and work area to work area. ☐

i People work best at simple, undemanding tasks, so it is best to break down jobs into small parts and cut out the need for people lower down the organization to make decisions. ☐

j People work best if they are given complete and meaningful jobs to do. With the right opportunities for training, most people can cope with more difficult and demanding work, so it is best to keep variety and flexibility in jobs. ☐

According to the experience of most successful organizations, the philosophy expressed by (b), (e), (f), (h) and (j) above are more likely to encourage a positive attitude to change than the philosophy suggested by (a), (c), (d), (g) and (i).

As a first line manager, it is your responsibility to ensure that your team have the necessary information, knowledge and skills to adapt to, and initiate, change. You also need to help them feel that they 'own' any change they are involved in implementing. If they see change as something imposed upon 'us' by 'them', they will find it much more difficult to be enthusiastic about it.

Ownership is the key to success in implementing change. Those who feel they own something are much more likely to take care of it.

## 2.1 Overcoming resistance to innovation and change in yourself

Before you can begin to overcome your own resistance to innovation and change, you need to think about the reasons for the resistance.

Activity 3 · 4 mins

Put yourself in the position of a manager whose team or department is being 'investigated' with a view to changing it. Why might you react in a negative way? What reasons might you have to fear change?

Spend a few minutes thinking about this and then write down your response briefly.

_____

_____

_____

_____

If you are like most people, you might well resent the interference of the investigation. But your reaction to what you see as the threat of change could be:

■ fear that you will lose your status or position;
■ worry that your career prospects will suffer;
■ anxiety about consequent loss of earnings.

You may see change as a threat to position, prospects or prosperity. In addition, you may feel:

- anger that all the work you have done to build up the present system may now be thrown away;
- that you aren't in control of your own destiny;
- general uncertainty.

## 2.2 Encouraging creativity and innovation

Creativity has been defined as 'the thinking of novel and appropriate ideas' and innovation as 'the successful implementation of those ideas within an organization'. These days the pace of change has placed a premium on the ability of organizations to think of novel and appropriate ideas and to implement these successfully. Those unable to do so will find themselves left behind as other organizations prove themselves able to do so. This is as true in the public and voluntary sectors as it is in the private sector.

You must take the lead with your team in encouraging them to think creatively and to welcome innovative change. This means being open to new ideas and looking at ways of making them work, not reasons for rejecting them. Whenever someone comes up with a new idea remember to say 'Yes and . . .' to find ways round barriers, not 'Yes but . . .' to put barriers up yourself. Remember, change is inevitable; survival is optional.

## 3 Acknowledging resistance to change in others

Apprehension and doubt about proposed changes are to be expected.

When faced with the prospect of change, people will often react by seeing it as a threat, especially when the implications of the change haven't been discussed with them, for example when a company announces a major change of policy and approach.

# Activity 4

6 mins

Imagine that your organization has announced a new 'customer awareness' programme, in the face of a growing number of customer complaints. The directors have made it clear that everyone will have to become more proactive in customer care. A series of seminars on the subject are to be held, which everyone will be expected to attend.

Your team normally has minimum contact with customers. Before the programme starts you talk to them about it to get their reactions. What sort of thing might they say? Write down two or three sentences of imagined conversations.

_____

_____

_____

_____

_____

_____

Here are some typical reactions.

- 'I hope this is not just another management gimmick.'
- 'This has nothing to do with us. We never see the customer.'
- 'I'm not a sales or marketing person. I'm not even very good at talking to people. How will I cope?'
- 'Will this mean that we all have to start wearing smart suits?'
- 'Will we now be judged on how well we can chat people up? I'm a specialist, not a salesperson.'
- 'Just when I'd got this job taped up, they want to change everything. Why can't things go on as they did before? I thought it was all going well.'

There is invariably an initial resistance to change. It's the kind of situation where, as a first line manager, you will need all your skills of tact and persuasion. In fact, you will need to think very carefully about how to introduce a programme for change to your team – something that the manager featured in the next Activity clearly failed to do.

# Activity 5 ·

3 mins

The workteam knew that their team leader, Piers Loman, had been attending an important meeting with senior management. When he came back to the shop floor, several of his team looked at him expectantly.

'I can't say anything except that there will be a lot of changes around here,' Piers said. 'You'll probably be told more next week.'

How do you think the team would react to a statement like that?

_____

_____

_____

It wouldn't be surprising if the team members stopped work, as soon as the leader's back was turned, to speculate about the possible changes. How could they be expected to concentrate with something like that hanging over their heads?

Unspecified changes will evoke strong emotions: often a mixture of anxiety, excitement and hope. Change is threatening – and at the same time offers new possibilities for the future.

Let's continue the story.

# Activity 6 ·

3 mins

The following week Piers gathered the workteam together and made an announcement.

'I can now reveal to you that the job we are currently doing will cease as from this Friday. But there's no need for any of you to be concerned. You will all be re-assigned to new duties. Of course, it will mean that many of you will have to be given training in new skills. Jean Winkler and I will be discussing your new jobs with you as soon as possible. Meanwhile, just relax and don't worry.'

How do you imagine that the team members will take Piers' last piece of advice? How do you think they will react now?

_____

_____

_____

_____

_____

> Not giving out information about a forthcoming change, or handing it out piecemeal, leads to great uncertainty in people. And this uncertainty is one of the main reasons for them feeling negative about the prospect of change.

If they had difficulty concentrating on their work after Piers' earlier remarks, the team members are now likely to have trouble sleeping at night as well! What the manager has just said is that the whole of their working lives will change – and he expects them to relax!

Let's be honest: this kind of situation is not exactly unknown, is it? In many companies, drastic changes are planned without consulting the people most affected by them. And information is handed out piecemeal, so provoking the kind of negative reactions they would prefer to avoid.

## Activity 7

5 mins

We've already discussed the fact that people need information. Piers Loman is apparently giving his team all the information he has, so where is he going wrong? What should he have done differently? Think this over for a few minutes and then write down your ideas.

_____

_____

_____

_____

_____

In fact, Piers has not really given very much in the way of useful information. He has let it be known that drastic changes are planned, which will affect the working lives of his team members. Without any information on just how each person will be affected, this is worse than knowing nothing.

It would have been better if Piers had said nothing – and preferably not have even disclosed at the start the fact that he was going to an important meeting.

Only when he had sat down with this manager (or whoever else was involved) and worked out what the main implications would be, should he have made any announcement. This is not withholding information – it is preparing information so that it can be used effectively.

Of course, he might have to act quickly.

## Activity 8 · 3 mins

Why might Piers have to work hard to get the details out quickly? What is the danger here?

_____

_____

_____

_____

The danger is that the rumours of impending change may get out before all the details can be prepared. In many places of work there is a 'grapevine' which is capable of spreading information and misinformation very quickly. Piers would be under great pressure if news of the proposals are 'leaked', because the rumours would tend to have a similar effect to a premature announcement.

These kinds of decisions are never easy: when to make announcements of change, what to say, who to tell first. They are not easy for any level of management. The important thing to bear in mind is that disturbing news is bound to upset people, so:

**it is important to think through the consequences of announcements about change.**

# 4 Managing resistance to change

We have seen that resistance to change is normal, and that its underlying causes are:

■ a perceived threat to position, prosperity or prospects;
■ the natural inclination to hang on to what you know, rather than embrace something that is unfamiliar;
■ uncertainty.

Normal as it is, this doesn't change the fact that you will often have to overcome resistance to change. So how do you go about doing this?

One of the first things you can do is to think carefully about the precise nature of the forces opposed to the change – and then identify those forces that are behind the change. Identifying these forces is what is known as a 'force field analysis'.

## 4.1 Force field analysis

Imagine the reactions of staff to the announcement of a new customer awareness programme. They might come up with the following objections, each of which could be seen as a force opposing change – for example:

■ the suspicion that this was just another management gimmick that would not amount to much in reality;
■ the feeling that the new programme had nothing to do with them as they rarely saw a customer;
■ the belief that they did not have sufficient marketing and selling skills to be able to contribute to the programme effectively;
■ a general fear of the unknown.

But these could be positive reactions as well, each of which could be seen as a force supporting change. They might have included:

■ the feeling among some staff that their jobs might become more interesting;
■ appreciation of the opportunity to acquire new knowledge and skills;
■ relief that something is going to be done about the increasing number of customer complaints.

Of course, the forces that will support or oppose a change do not only reflect the attitudes of staff. There are other forces that come from both within and outside the organization. In our example, the supporting forces include the growing number of customer complaints and the decision of management to introduce a new customer care programme. The opposing forces include the disruption caused by staff attending a series of seminars.

Once you have considered what the 'supporting' and 'opposing' forces are, the next step is to map out these forces in a diagram, such as the one below. Begin by drawing a horizontal line. Next, list the supporting forces above the line and the opposing forces below the line. If possible, draw arrows of varying thickness to indicate the comparative strength of each force.

**Supporting Forces**

| Determination of directors to introduce programme | Growing number of customer complaints | Relief that action is to be taken | Appreciation of opportunity to learn new skills | Belief among staff that job interest will increase |
|---|---|---|---|---|
| ⬇ | ⬇ | ⬇ | ⬇ | ⬇ |

—————————————————————————————————————

| ⬆ | ⬆ | ⬆ | ⬆ | ⬆ |
|---|---|---|---|---|
| Suspicion that it is a management gimmick | Disruption caused by seminars | Feeling among some staff that programme is nothing to do with them | Belief among staff that they lack necessary skills | General fear of the unknown |

**Opposing Forces**

Once you have produced this diagram you can start thinking about ways of:

- maintaining the supporting forces at their present level;
- reducing the opposing forces.

What you definitely shouldn't do is ignore the opposing forces and just concentrate on further strengthening the supporting forces. If you do, you will probably end up increasing resistance! Returning to our example, if management were to react to grumbles among the staff by simply repeating their determination to introduce the customer awareness programme, this would only increase the grumbles.

## Activity 9

If you were the manager of a team who had just been told about a new customer awareness programme, what would you do to reduce the opposing forces?

_____

_____

_____

_____

You might stress that management were actually concerned about the level of customer complaints and were serious about improving customer care. You might point out that customer care is a lot more than speaking politely to customers: that it's fundamentally about ensuring that customer needs are met through improving the quality of products or services while continuing to provide them at a price the customers can afford. This means that you don't have to have everyday contact with customers in order to contribute to customer care. You might also emphasize that staff will be equipped with any necessary new skills through training and that the programme represents an opportunity for all staff to expand their jobs and make them more interesting. There are many positive elements in change, including the fact that it brings new challenges and new interest to a job.

## Activity 10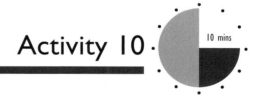

**S/NVQ C6**

This Activity may provide the basis of appropriate evidence for your S/NVQ portfolio. If you are intending to take this course of action, it might be better to write your answer on separate sheets of paper.

Think about a significant change in which you and your team have recently been involved.

What would you say were the forces supporting change?

_____

_____

_____

What were the forces opposing change?

_____

_____

_____

What, if anything, did you do to maintain the supporting forces and decrease the opposing forces?

_____

_____

_____

Thinking about the change again, what more might you have done in response to the opposing forces?

_____

_____

_____

_____

## 4.2 Unfreezing, movement and refreezing

The stage during which you identify and work on the forces for and against change, and so create a climate in which change can more easily take place, is often called 'unfreezing'. Put another way, unfreezing 'warms people up' to the idea of change. During this stage it is essential to have two-way communication, in which you discuss with people:

■ why the proposed change is necessary – that is, what problems the change is intended to solve;

■ the benefits of the change;

■ what new skills the change will give staff the opportunity to acquire.

You also need to give people the opportunity to talk about their worries and provide them with reassurance.

Once people have got used to the idea of change, you are ready to progress to the movement stage, when change actually begins to happen. The key to success in this stage is ensuring that people have a sense of ownership. This means giving them the opportunity to **participate** in the planning of how the change is to be implemented. It also means giving them the **information**, knowledge and skills they need to handle the change. Finally, to implement change successfully you need to demonstrate **enthusiasm.**

You can remember the three main ingredients of the recipe for successful change implementation by the letters PIE.

■ Participation

■ Information

■ Enthusiasm

Once the change has taken place we come to the refreezing stage, when people settle down into the new way of doing things. We'll return to the stage of refreezing at the end of this session, but first we're going to look in more detail at PIE.

# 4.3 Participation

Activity 11

Suppose your team has been assigned some new equipment to help you do your job more efficiently. The equipment is due to arrive in a month's time. Your main concern is that the team members will have to change their ways of working, learn how to use the equipment, but continue to be a productive unit during the period of change-over.

You decide that your first priority is to get every team member thinking in a positive way about the change.

How would you approach this task? Jot down your thoughts briefly.

_____

_____

_____

_____

One approach is to describe the equipment to the team and point out that it is designed to make the job easier. This would certainly help to overcome any scepticism – people are obviously much happier to accept a change if they see it as helping to lessen their workload.

However, the worth of the equipment has yet to be proven, so it may be seen as just another problem. A way to overcome this is to invite the team to participate in planning for the change. If people are involved in solving a mutual problem, they tend to concentrate on helping each other, rather than worrying about the effects on them personally.

How you go about this will depend on you and your team. You might feel it best to start by holding a general discussion, with you standing at a blackboard or flip-chart, writing down the points as they arise. The starting point could be: 'This is the new equipment. It looks like it could be useful to us. What we have to decide is how to get the most from it without letting it disrupt our normal work. I need your ideas. In fact, I will need you to organize the whole business.'

Or you might involve more senior members of the team first, perhaps putting the problem as 'How do we get these youngsters to cope with the new equipment?'

You know your team best, and what they are capable of, so there is no single approach that will work in all circumstances. One thing is certain, however:

**where change is concerned, participation is the best antidote to resistance.**

# 4.4 Information

As has been suggested before, one of the main causes of negative and emotional reactions to change is uncertainty.

The best cure for the anguish of uncertainty is information.

Projected change provokes questions. If the questions go unanswered, they become problems; and the problems, real or imagined, will undermine the effectiveness of the plans.

## Activity 12

Suppose you are in charge of the day-to-day running of a branch of a building society. The management have found new premises in the town and you are made responsible for planning and organizing the move. You are determined to keep the team fully informed, so as to avoid problems arising from uncertainty.

What actions could you take to do this effectively? Think about this for a few minutes, then write down at least three things that you might do.

_____

_____

_____

_____

_____

Some ways of keeping the team informed during a move, would be to:

■ show them the new premises, collectively and/or individually: where they will work, the facilities available and so on;

■ hold a meeting in which you announce details of the move, followed by a discussion session in which you do your best to answer any questions that arise;

■ extend an invitation to all members of the team to discuss privately any particular problems they foresee, so you can try to overcome them together and allay any fears;

■ make it clear to each person what part they have to play during the changeover, including what they should tell their customers and so on.

**Information is the best medicine for uncertainty.**

# 4.5 Enthusiasm

It almost goes without saying that the team leader has to try to inspire enthusiasm, because enthusiasm helps smooth out the snags.

If the team members see that their leader is lukewarm and half-hearted about the proposals for change, they will tend to act in the same way.

Leaders of change who show fire and fervour are likely to carry the team along with them.

**Enthusiasm is infectious.**

Of course, in reality it is sometimes hard to be enthusiastic. What do you do if you have serious misgivings about a proposed change, or the way you've been told it is to be implemented?

# Activity 13

Imagine your company announces a new bonus scheme to replace an earlier one. You, along with other first line managers, are told about this and instructed to pass on details to your team. Initially, you sit down and work out that your team will be worse off than before, whereas most other teams will benefit from the new scheme.

What can you do? How can you go along to your team and enthusiastically announce the scheme knowing that your group will be out of pocket? Think about how you would handle a situation like this.

Which of the following would you do?

- Pretend to your team that there really is no difference between the two schemes?
- Blame it all on management and say that it isn't your fault?
- Ask for an urgent discussion with your manager to point out the problem and ask for some changes to the scheme?
- Go to your manager and say that it's up to him or her to tell the team, as you don't want to be the unpopular one?
- Take some other action (write down your ideas here)?

_____

_____

_____

_____

Your options may be limited but you at least have to explore them all. What you **can't** do is go along to the team and say: 'Management have really done it to us this time!' because team morale will sink to rock bottom and create a rift in the company that may be hard to repair. Team leaders have to represent the workteam appropriately to management, and management properly to the team, or nothing they try to achieve will work well.

Also, there's no point in pretending that there isn't a problem. People are very quick to realize that their income has been reduced, and then you would either look foolish or dishonest – or both.

Your best option in this case may be to request an urgent discussion of the matter with your manager, in which you point out the negative effects of the change, and perhaps ask whether your team can be compensated for their losses in some way. You might even propose an alternative scheme or a modification to the proposals. After all, the idea of bonus schemes is to provide an incentive to work harder. It isn't in the company's interests for them to have the opposite effect.

There are other kinds of situations where you may not agree with the changes proposed, yet accept the fact that they are inevitable. A company that is losing money may have to make some personnel redundant, for instance, or even close a part of its operation. These changes are always hard to face, and enthusiasm doesn't come into it. The best you can do is try to soften the blow as much as circumstances allow.

EXTENSION 1
A useful guide to leading teams through the process of change is provided by extension 2, *Handbook for Creative Team Leaders* by Tudor Rickards and Susan Moger.

Once you have explored every aspect of the change proposals with which you disagree, and have done all you can to put forward your own and your team's point of view, then all that is left is:

**to be as positive and open-minded as you can.**

## 4.6 The refreezing stage

The term 'refreezing' might imply to you that once you have gone through a period of change, everything settles down again into a new stable situation. In fact, this isn't quite true. As change is a constant feature of life, no one can expect that once a change has taken place there won't be another. However, the refreezing stage acknowledges that it always takes time for people to become accustomed to using new skills and knowledge and practising new ways of working. You can't necessarily expect the same level of efficiency and performance straight away.

# Activity 14

As a first line manager, you need to be alert to any problems arising from the implementation of change, and take whatever steps you can to minimize them. Which of the following courses of action do you think would be most suitable during the refreezing stage? Tick more than one box if you wish.

a  Being receptive to feedback, as you want to get the team involved.  ❑

b  Not taking too much notice of comments, on the grounds that all changes are bound to bring a few grumbles.  ❑

c  Insisting that everything is done as was originally planned.  ❑

d  Being prepared to make adjustments to the original plan for change in the light of experience and new knowledge.  ❑

e  Seeking the opinions of the workteam on the effects of the change.  ❑

EXTENSION 2
You will find an overview of the many aspects of organizational change in extension 2, *Managing Change* by Robert Heller.

(a), (d) and (e) are probably the most appropriate and effective way to behave. Plans are seldom put into effect without modification, because it is very difficult for planners to foresee all the consequences of the change. During the refreezing stage, snags and problems will inevitably arise. As a leader of change, you need to watch out for these, listen to the comments of team members and be prepared to make adjustments.

Being a leader of change requires the ability to be flexible.

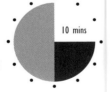

# Self-assessment 1

1  In each of the following statements, pick the one word or phrase that is the most suitable.
a  Resistance to change is INAPPROPRIATE/DESIRABLE/NORMAL.
b  People often resist change because of GENERAL UNCERTAINTY/ CERTAINTY THAT IT WILL MAKE THINGS WORSE.
c  As a manager you should focus on how to respond to proposals for change in a QUESTIONING/DIPLOMATIC/CONSTRUCTIVE way.

2   The missing word in the following statement begins with P. What is it?

Among the main underlying causes of people's resistance to change is that they see it as a threat to their position, prospects and _____.

3   In any change situation, there will be forces supporting and forces opposing the change. When faced with forces opposed to change, which **two** of the following should you do?

■ Increase the supporting forces.
■ Maintain the supporting forces at their present level.
■ Reduce the opposing forces.
■ Ignore the opposing forces.

4   Fill in the missing words.

a Where change is concerned, _____ is the best antidote to resistance.

b _____ is the best medicine for uncertainty.

c _____ is infectious.

| | | |
|---|---|---|
| INFORMATION | PLANNING | ENTHUSIASM |
| CHANGE | PARTICIPATION | ASSERTIVENESS |

Answers to these questions can be found on page 81.

# 5 Summary

- Resistance to change is normal.

- When you react negatively to the prospect of change, it may be because you see it as a threat to position, prospects or prosperity, or because you are uncertain about what it will bring.

- As a manager, you need to take the lead in overcoming your initial negative reactions to proposals for change and focus on how to respond in a constructive way.

- Before announcing any major change, it is essential to know what the main implications of that change will be.

- In any change situation, there will be forces supporting and forces opposing the change. As a leader of change, you need to work on maintaining the forces that support a change and reducing those that oppose it.

- Two-way communication has a major role to play in preparing people for change during the 'unfreezing stage' of a change programme.

- The three main ingredients of the recipe for successful change implementation are as follows.
  - Participation
  - Information
  - Enthusiasm

- Where change is concerned, participation is the best antidote to resistance.

- Information is the best medicine for uncertainty arising from change.

- In reality, it is sometimes hard to be enthusiastic. In situations where you do not agree with the proposed changes that you have been asked to implement, you may have to settle for being as positive and open-minded as you can.

- During the 'refreezing' stage, you need to:
  - be receptive to feedback from the team;
  - be prepared to make adjustments to the original plan;
  - seek the opinions of your team on the effects of the change.

# Session B
## Planning change

## 1 Introduction

In the first session we looked at some of the barriers you will meet in implementing change. Recognizing that these will exist and that they have to be overcome is essential if the change is to happen successfully. So too is planning. Change has to be planned very carefully if it is to be successful. As a first line manager you have an important part to play in this process, ensuring that objectives are set, actions to achieve these objectives are identified and assigned to the most appropriate members of staff, and that results are monitored against the objectives.

We will be examining this planning process in some detail. But first we are going to consider the nature of major change and the reasons for it.

## ▣ 2 Reasons for major change

Activity 15

5 mins

Think back over your own working life and/or that of other members of your family or friends. What major changes have occurred in the organizations you or they have worked for? Jot down two or three.

_____

_____

_____

In almost any organization there's a good chance that major change has taken place in recent years in one or more of the following ways:

■ the development of a totally new product or service;
■ a significant expansion or reduction of the workforce;
■ a merger with, or a take-over of/by another organization;
■ restructuring to eliminate layers of management and/or create new departmental boundaries;
■ the relocation of premises.

The ultimate aim of any commercial organization in making such a major change is to increase its profits. But the precise nature of the change will depend on a number of factors, both within and outside the organization. As in the case of small-scale gradual change, internal factors include the need for improvements in physical conditions, resources (including finance), staff skills, relationships and procedures. Factors within the external environment may be of a political, economic, social, technological, legal or environmental nature.

■ **Political factors**
The nature of the government and the policies it pursues can have a major impact on organizations. Just one example is the introduction in 2001 of the Climate Change Levy, a tax on businesses which is designed to encourage them to reduce their energy consumption. Such a tax reflects the government's growing concern over the need to reduce the consumption of finite resources, and it means that manufacturers, in particular, need to find ways of using energy more efficiently.

■ **Economic factors**

Some developments in the economy are dictated by government policies, notably measures announced in the annual budget. Others are outside the government's control. The discovery in 2002, for example, that large American corporations such as Enron and WorldCom had claimed to have made huge profits when in fact they had made none, led to a dramatic drop in the value of almost all organizations' shares on both the American and UK stock markets.

■ **Social factors**

Among the long-term social factors that have had a major impact in recent years is the ageing of the population coupled with the growing power of the youth market. Among the more short-term social factors are changing fashions in such things as clothes and food.

■ **Technological factors**

Personal computers, mobile phones and the Internet – all are among the numerous technological developments that have created big changes in people's lives, and in the way organizations function, as well as in the goods and services they offer.

■ **Legal factors**

Laws and regulations, whether they be at local, national or European level, affect organizations in numerous ways. They range from measures to protect employees and consumers to measures aimed at controlling all aspects of an organization's activities. Just one simple example is a planned European regulation for scrapped cars to be returned to the manufacturers, thus putting pressure on them to produce cars whose parts can be recycled.

■ **Environmental factors**

The planned European regulation on cars is a reflection of the growing concern with environmental factors. These fall into two categories:

- those concerning pollution of the Earth and its atmosphere by all forms of waste, ranging from gases to oil rigs;
- those concerning the over-exploitation of the Earth's finite resources.

Concern over environmental factors has resulted in many laws and regulations that affect the activities of organizations. It has also created many opportunities for organizations, such as The Body Shop and its competitors, to develop new products for consumers who wish to purchase goods that use natural, replaceable resources and recyclable packaging.

All the various types of factor discussed above can represent both threats and opportunities to an organization. Either way, any organization that chooses to ignore them, and not change, will lose out in the end.

# 3 Change and the first line manager

Major changes at work do not simply happen: they are made to work by people. The job of managers is to give the lead to their teams. This does not mean that people have to be told exactly what to do and when and how to do it. The primary skill of leading and managing is to find ways of gaining:

- influence;
- trust and respect;
- voluntary co-operation;
- commitment to the task.

First line managers are very often put under pressure before anyone else by senior management's requirements for change. Higher management may make plans for the organization as a whole, but more often than not it is the first line manager who has to turn these plans into reality.

## Activity 16

15 mins

**S/NVQ
C6**

This Activity may provide the basis of appropriate evidence for your S/NVQ portfolio. If you are intending to take this course of action, it might be better to write your answers on separate sheets of paper.

Before we continue this session, think about your own work situation, and if possible identify two fairly major changes, one which you have already experienced, and one which you expect could happen in the near future.

In each case, briefly describe the change.

a What was the event that has already taken place? What contribution did you and your team make to it?

_____

_____

_____

_____

_____

_____

_____

_____

_____

_____

You will need your answer to Activity 16a for Activities 17, 18, 19, 30 and 34. You will need your answer to Activity 16b for Activities 21, 23, 24, 28 and 29.

b  What is the change that you expect to be involved in shortly? Explain how you and your team plan to play your part in its implementation.

_____

_____

_____

_____

_____

_____

_____

_____

_____

_____

_____

## 3.1  The first line manager as an instigator of change

In many organizations, plans for change that will affect more than one team are instigated by the higher levels of management. However, this need not always be the case, as the following example illustrates.

> On a construction site for a complex of large buildings, Michael was manager of the wall-building team. One of the things about his job that had often annoyed him in the past was that the team who installed the ducting, through which the wiring passed in the ceiling area, always worked ahead of his team. This meant that when his team came to build a wall, they had to spend at least half a day making fine adjustments to its design, and then implementing these adjustments, to take account of where the ducting was positioned. This often meant working for a long time on a ladder supported by scaffolding, with your head back. This was not only uncomfortable but an incredible waste of

time. Michael thought there had to be a better way of doing this and decided to talk to the site planner, who was responsible for sorting out the sequencing of work. The site planner agreed he had a point and suggested that a meeting be arranged which was to be attended by herself, Michael, the manager of the ducting team, and at least one building designer.

It quickly became apparent during this meeting that the designers did not always know exactly where the interior walls were going to go once the outer shell of the building had been constructed. Sometimes this outer shell had been erected just a few centimetres to the side of its planned position, but this did not mean that the designers then recalculated the positions of the interior walls. Neither they nor the planner had any idea of the importance for the teams doing the actual construction of knowing the exact position of the interface between the ducting and walls.

After much discussion and drawing of alternative process flowcharts on a whiteboard, it was agreed that in future the main stages of the process for installing walls and ducting should be as follows:

1 Once shell is in place, designer to establish whether it accords exactly with drawings and make any necessary amendments to drawings.

2 Designer to mark out on floor exactly where walls should go.

3 Plumb lines to be dropped from ceiling to exact points on floor where walls are to go, thus locating exact position of interfaces between walls and ducting.

4 Work on construction of walls to proceed before ducting is installed. Once a wall is approaching ceiling area, members of walling team to take a piece of rectangular ducting and install it within top of wall.

5 Once all interfaces between walls and length of ducting have been constructed, ducting team to install remainder of ducting.

When the various people involved in this process tried it out over the course of the next few weeks, they found that the job of installing a piece of ducting in the top of a wall took about 30 minutes. This compared exceedingly well with the half-day it had previously taken for the walling team to do the best they could with the ducting that was already in place. In a building with six walls this represented a saving in time of at least 18 hours – which in turn represented a big financial saving for the construction company.

In this example, just one small idea for change had important implications for a number of different people and the organization they worked for. In looking for ways of improving processes, products and services, you too may come up with ideas that have important implications for your organization and require you to work with other managers. Why not seize the initiative and voice your ideas to your manager? You may need permission to put the change into effect, but your idea and enterprise will almost certainly stand you in good stead.

## Activity 17 · 3 mins

S/NVQ
C6

Take a look at your description of a change in Activity 16a. Was it one that you helped to instigate, or was it imposed on you by senior management? Whatever your answer, what do you think was the main reason for the change? Was it, for example, made in response to economic factors in the external environment, or in response to something within the organization, such as the inefficient use of resources?

_____

_____

_____

_____

Whether or not external forces for change played a part in prompting the change you have described, you should bear in mind that as a manager you should always be aware of such forces – be they economic, social, technological, political, legal or environmental.

## 3.2 Other elements in the first line manager's role

As well as instigating change, your role as a first line manager in change will encompass:

■ **calculating costs**
You may simply be presented with a budget to manage. Alternatively, you may be asked to estimate costs of particular actions or processes.

■ **determining feasibility**

You and your fellow first line managers are often in the best position to know whether a proposal will work, or is achievable within a certain timescale or cost limit.

■ **feeding back information**

Your experience and your team may be key to the project, and you will be expected to contribute information to support the decisions made by your line managers and others.

# Activity 18

**S/NVQ C6**

This Activity may provide the basis of appropriate evidence for your S/NVQ portfolio. If you are intending to take this course of action, it might be better to write your answers on separate sheets of paper.

Looking back at the change in Activity 16a, describe how you gave feedback to your team which resulted in a modification to a planned change. Alternatively, choose another occasion when you gave feedback to your team, which resulted in the modification of plans.

_____

_____

_____

_____

_____

_____

_____

_____

_____

_____

Other elements in your role as leader of change may include:

■ **working out a strategy for deployment of staff**

Staff deployment is usually part of the first line manager's day-to-day job. Where substantial changes are underway, this aspect of the work can become more difficult than usual.

- **'selling' the idea of change to the team**

  To sell something, whether it is a product, a process or an idea, it is necessary to persuade potential buyers that they will benefit from the exchange. In this case, the workteam will pay you in their commitment to the project.

- **empowering the workteam to cope with the change**

  It is not enough to sell the idea. You must empower your workteam to manage things in their own way. More and more, organizations are realizing that the old ways of managing by telling people what to do and how to do it are no longer appropriate. As competition gets more fierce, greater commitment is needed from staff at all levels. The only way to achieve this is by allowing increased levels of freedom for people to organize their own work – to hand over control of tasks to those who have to accomplish them.

  Handing over more authority to your team is a courageous step. It involves watching them learn from their mistakes. It cannot be taken lightly. If and when you do it, the workteam will certainly depend on your full trust and support.

  You will also have to provide them with the practical resources and training they need beforehand.

## Activity 19

S/NVQ
C6

This Activity may provide the basis of appropriate evidence for your S/NVQ portfolio. If you are intending to take this course of action, it might be better to write your answers on separate sheets of paper.

For the project you described in Activity 16a, describe the recommendations you made, and the steps you took, to provide the workteam with the necessary resources, (perhaps) including training.

_____

_____

_____

_____

_____

Continuing our discussion of your role as leader of change, your tasks should include:

■ **providing your team with the feeling of ownership of the change**
Once you have sold the idea of the change, you can complete the deal by handing over the ownership. Your team will be a lot more committed to the change if they feel they are controlling the action themselves and are:

- not being kept in the dark;
- not simply looking on from the sidelines;
- not just helping implement the plans of management.

If you can manage to do this, they will become enthusiastic about the change, and promote it to others.

■ **keeping the team informed**
It is essential that you keep the team informed throughout all stages of the change process, from the time you announce the change to your final evaluation of what the change has achieved. You'll find more on this subject in the next section.

■ **coping with keeping things running during the change**
This may be your greatest challenge.

## 3.3  Keeping the team informed

In implementing change, the keys to success include empowering your team to cope with the change and giving them a sense of ownership, thus ensuring their full **participation** in the change process. Another key to success is ensuring that your team always receives sufficient **information**. Finally, there is the need for you to inspire **enthusiasm** by being enthusiastic yourself whenever possible. Here we are going to focus on the importance of keeping your team informed right from the beginning of any change programme.

# Activity 20

5 mins

At the HiPrint works, there was a lot of discussion going on. It was a well-known fact that the company had been looking for new premises for some time. A few months previously, a lot of the staff had expressed concern that the company would move away from the town – perhaps to one of those remote government development areas – and that everyone would be given the choice of moving house or finding a new job. But nothing seemed to come of the idea and the workforce more or less forgot about it.

Now the rumour was going around that a new site had been found, five miles on the other side of town. As you can imagine, a lot of questions were being asked.

What do you think the main concerns of the workforce would be? Write down **three** or **four** questions that might be going through their minds.

_____

_____

_____

_____

_____

_____

They would probably be asking questions like:

'Will any of us lose our jobs through the move – perhaps they'll try to recruit people in the local area?'

'How will I get to work? Is there a bus service? Will the company provide a company bus?'

'Will it mean that we'll have to get up earlier, or get home later?'

'Will we be paid compensation?'

'Will it be more – or less – pleasant to work in?'

'If there are bigger premises, will there now be room for a canteen?'

In short, every member of the workforce will want to know:

'How will the change affect me? Will it bring new problems and how will I deal with them? Will it perhaps bring new opportunities?'

If you've ever been involved in a major change like moving premises, you will know something of the headaches it brings. For the first line manager, it can mean a hundred new problems, often compounded by the fact that management insist on minimum work being lost during the move.

For the team member, the worries are more personal. The greatest fear in any upheaval is job loss. After that, the concern will be over money, disturbance, intrusion and inconvenience. These anxieties are in addition to the unease felt about changes related to the job itself. The effects of all these cares may be to cause:

- emotional outbursts;
- unreasonable and unreasoning behaviour;

- lowering of work performance;
- sickness or other absence;
- argument and other conflict.

Once all the uncertainty has been resolved, most of the worries disappear and the mood changes – even before the change takes place.

**It isn't change that creates the anxiety so much as uncertainty about change. And to avoid uncertainty, you need to provide information.**

# 4 Preparing for change

The period in which you prepare people for change is often referred to as the 'unfreezing' stage. Of course, you can't embark on this until you yourself know what form the change is going to take. There is nothing more likely to cause mounting levels of anxiety than making an announcement that there is going to be change and then not saying anything more about it. So the first thing you need to do in any major change is to define its scope – that is, produce a broad outline of what it will involve.

## 4.1 Defining the scope of change

When considering a major change, it is useful to think of it as a project, or even as a number of projects. Doing this will help you to define the scope of the change, as in the following example.

Stella was the manager of a long-established health club which was beginning to lose clients to a new club that had opened up a couple of miles away. From talking to the reception staff about various comments made by clients, she knew there had been several causes for complaint, including:

- changing and shower facilities not always as clean as they might be;
- pieces of equipment in the gym often faulty or broken down completely;
- general lack of interest among staff in client progress with exercise regimes in the gym;
- bottlenecks for various items of apparatus at most popular times;
- reception and café areas not very inviting;

- insufficient number of yoga classes;
- teachers not always turning up for their classes.

Clearly a major overhaul of the club was necessary if it was to stop losing clients and attract new ones. It was going to require some investment from the owners, training for the staff in the fundamentals of client care, and some reorganization of the way various things – such as the cleaning and maintenance of the equipment in the gym – were done. And once all the improvements had been made they would have to be publicized in order to attract new clients.

It was a lot of work for one person to manage while still keeping the club running as efficiently as possible on a day-to-day basis. Stella decided that the only way to handle it was to think of the work as five sub-projects and delegate responsibility for them to five sub-teams:

- redesigning the reception area and café;
- getting procedures and rotas for general maintenance and cleaning sorted out;
- establishing what classes should be run when, and identifying possible teachers;
- sorting out how the gym was run;
- organizing and distributing a publicity brochure.

Having got this far, Stella was well on the way to defining the project's scope and putting this in the form of a proposal to the club's owner. But first she needed to establish:

- who was going to be in the project team (or sub-teams);
- the project's aims and objectives;
- the approximate timescale and budget.

For Stella, deciding who was going to be in the team was easy: it had to be her whole team, which was all 12 full-time members of staff. She hoped that involving everyone in this way would actually be a first step to getting them more committed to the club and more prepared to look after the clients properly. However, drawing up the list of aims and objectives, and working out the approximate timescale and budget, was more problematic. She didn't think that she yet had sufficient information to do this properly. She would have to hold some meetings with her team, and possibly collect more data on what clients actually wanted, before she could complete her proposal.

# Activity 21

**S/NVQ C6**

This Activity may provide the basis of appropriate evidence for your S/NVQ portfolio. If you are intending to take this course of action, it might be better to write your answers on separate sheets of paper.

Look back at the change you described in Activity 16b. How would you define its scope? Is it possible to think of it as a number of sub-projects? If so, what are they?

_____

_____

_____

_____

## 4.2 Establishing aims and objectives

The importance of getting the objectives clear before the start of a change project can never be over-emphasized. If you don't know what you're aiming for, it's hard to achieve it. However, to be realistic, at the start of a project you may only be able to sketch out your main aims. You will then have to refine these at a later stage.

When producing your objectives you will find it helpful to bear in mind the SMART principle, which means that they are:

■ Specific – they state precisely what is to be achieved;
■ Measurable – their achievement is easy to assess;
■ Achievable – they can be attained given the current situation and the available skills and resources;
■ Relevant – they are of significance to the organization;
■ Time bound – the state precisely when something is to be achieved.

# Activity 22

5 mins

Thinking back to Stella and the health club, she might have said that one of her broad aims was to improve the level of cleanliness in the changing and shower areas. Can you suggest how this might have been rephrased as a SMART objective?

_____

_____

_____

Of course, there are numerous possible answers to this question. The following objective is just one of them: 'Within one month, establish a system for regular checking that the changing and shower areas are clear of litter and dirt, and for ensuring that these areas are cleaned thoroughly at least twice a day.' This assumes that there are sufficient staff to carry out this amount of checking and cleaning. If there are not, then the objective is not achievable.

Whatever the objectives of the project, it is best to agree them with the people involved wherever possible. However, you shouldn't expect to stick rigidly to this rule. If management has instigated the change, the objectives may be defined already, although they may need to be modified in some way. And it may not be wise to get the team involved in setting objectives if the project is going to lead to redundancies. (We will return to the subject of redundancies in Session C.) You will have to make up your own mind about the most appropriate time at which to get your team involved, depending on the situation.

# Activity 23

10 mins

**S/NVQ C6**

This Activity may provide the basis of appropriate evidence for your S/NVQ portfolio. If you are intending to take this course of action, it might be better to write your answers on separate sheets of paper.

Return to the change project you outlined in Activity 16b. Does the project have stated aims and objectives? If so, how might they be modified to take account of your team's particular circumstances or to make them more

SMART? If there are not stated aims or objectives, what suggestions do you have on what they should be?

_____

_____

_____

_____

_____

_____

_____

# 4.3 Establishing timescale and budget

At the outset of a change project it may only be possible to give a very approximate idea of the timescale and budget. And even when you have worked these out – or they've been worked out for you by senior management – it may, in fact, be necessary to carry out a feasibility study before you begin any serious planning.

The purpose of a feasibility study is to establish whether the desired outcomes of the project can be achieved within the available time and resources, most notably the budget and staff. When carrying out a feasibility study it is often very useful to include a cost-benefit analysis. This is discussed in some detail in the workbook entitled _Managing Projects_. In this workbook we will note simply that financial costs are often divided into two main categories:

- development costs – that is, the costs of the actual project;
- operational costs – that is, the running costs after the project has been completed.

Benefits are also often divided into two categories: financial and non-financial. In the case of Stella and the health club, for example, the intended main financial benefit of the change project is obviously increased revenue from an increasing number of clients. Non-financial benefits could include a more motivated staff, leading to improved quality of service, which in turn should help to increase the number of clients.

# Activity 24

This Activity may provide the basis of appropriate evidence for your S/NVQ portfolio. If you are intending to take this course of action, it might be better to write your answers on separate sheets of paper.

Returning to the change project outlined in Activity 16b, consider the following questions:

a  What is the proposed timescale?

Does the timescale appear reasonable? Is it feasible? If you don't think it is, what can you do about this?

_____

_____

b  What are the financial constraints?

Do you have a budget for the part of the change project for which you are responsible? If so, do you think it is enough? If you don't think it's enough, do you at least have a rough idea of how much you need?

_____

_____

c  Which people are available to help you in both the planning and implementation stages? And how much of their time will you require?

Is it the same group of people for both, or are there people who may be involved in one stage but not the other? Are there people, for example, from other teams or departments who need to be consulted in the planning stage but do not need to be involved in actual implementation?

_____

_____

d  What other resources (apart from finance and people) do you need in both stages?

_____

_____

You may have found it very difficult to answer these questions. It's not until you begin the detailed planning of a project that you begin to see exactly how long it is likely to take, and how much staff time and other resources you will need.

In practice you are sometimes given a date by which a project has to be completed and you then have to work backwards from that in your planning, rather than the other way round. You may also have to plan around the staff who are available to help – and the number of hours they are able to devote to your project – rather than beginning with your ideal requirements.

# 5 Planning the project activities

Once you have established the aims and objectives of the change project you need to set about planning exactly how you are going to achieve them – that is, establishing the key project activities and the order in which they should be completed. If you have not been able to do so before, this is certainly the point at which you need to involve your team.

There are a number of tools you and your team may find very useful in planning the project activities. The main ones are:

- logic diagrams;
- critical path diagrams;
- Gantt charts.

## 5.1 Logic diagrams

Constructing a logic diagram will help you to identify the key stages in the project and the order in which they should occur. Begin by establishing with your team what the main activities in the project will be: first write everyone's ideas on a whiteboard or flipchart and then decide what the main activities actually are. You don't want to end up with an unmanageable number. You can then write each activity on a sticky-note or piece of adhesive coloured card and arrange these on the flipchart or board until you have them in a logical order. The final step is to draw the diagram with arrows between the stages.

To return to Stella and the health club. The additional data she collected on clients' wants revealed that in addition to more yoga classes, they also wanted classes in Pilates and the Alexander technique.

The clients also had a lot to say about how the gym was run. For a start, they didn't like the way there were bottlenecks for some pieces of equipment during peak times. But more fundamental was the feeling that no one on the staff took a personal interest in them once their initial exercise regime had been established at the beginning of the year.

Finally, there was the café. Not only did they want the décor to be improved, they also wanted a better selection of drinks and snacks.

Stella produced a proposal taking all the new data into account and she secured the go-ahead from the owner. During discussions of the proposal with the staff, it was decided that the main activities were as follows:

A   Draw up detailed proposals for redesign of reception area and café.
B   Consult with clients on their views about designs and amend accordingly.
C   Organize redecoration and installation of new furniture.
D   Consult with clients on drinks and snacks they want in café.
E   Organize deliveries of requested drinks and snacks.
F   Establish procedures for checking state of changing and shower facilities, and cleaning during day.
G   Draw up rota for checking and cleaning procedures.
H   Establish procedures for checking equipment in gym every day and arranging for any broken equipment to be repaired.
I   Draw up rota for checking equipment.
J   Draw up new list of classes.
K   Consult with clients on list of classes to establish best times plus level of demand.
L   Recruit teachers for classes.
M   Organize and run client care session for teachers to stress importance of turning up on time and being well-prepared.
N   Set up appointments system for gym during peak periods (lunchtimes and evenings).
O   Organize client care session for all non-teaching staff, with emphasis on how to look after clients in gym.
P   Run client care sessions.
Q   Establish system for ensuring that clients in gym receive personal attention from one staff member throughout the year.
R   Organize publicity brochure.
S   Distribute publicity brochure.

# Activity 25

3 mins

In the list above:

- Which activities could be combined?

_____

- Which activities should, ideally, be carried out first, in parallel with each other?

_____

Activities B, D and K, all of which involve consulting with clients, could be carried out at the same time. So too, perhaps, could Activities M and O, both of which are concerned with giving staff training in client care.

Activities A, F, H, J and N should all, ideally, be carried out first in parallel with each other. (R – Organize publicity brochure – is another possibility, but it's probably best to produce this after the consultation exercise has been completed.) Whether this is actually possible in practice will depend on the number of staff available. It would be no good getting so many staff involved in the change project at any one time that they couldn't continue with the day-to-day work of running the club at least to present standards.

In fact, Stella and her team decided that they could carry out A, F, H, J and N in parallel, and so ended up with the logic diagram on the next page.

There are a number of things to notice about this diagram:

- The diagram begins with 'Start' and ends with 'Finish'.
- The arrows show which activities are dependent on other activities.
- There is no timescale.
- No activities are assigned to people.

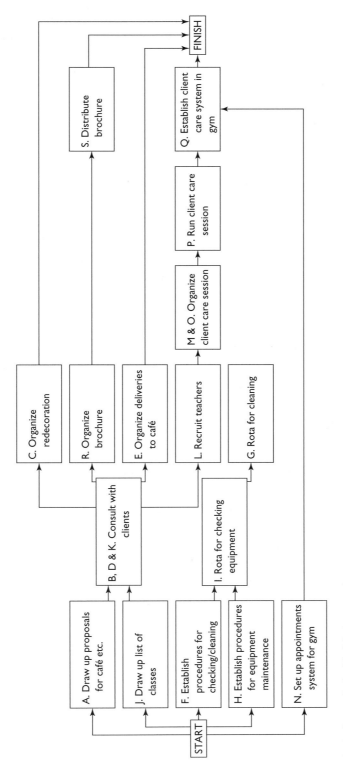

Logic diagram for health club change project

# 5.2 Critical path diagrams

A critical path diagram is a useful tool for estimating precisely the time a change project will take, and drawing up a schedule. A critical path diagram (also known as a network analysis) is a useful tool for doing this, as it shows how long individual activities should take and the relationship between them.

Let's first assume you haven't been given a completion date that you must achieve. The first step is to look at each of the main activities included in your logic diagram and decide with your team:

- what the activity consists of and how long it will take;
- which staff should carry it out;
- given the existing workload of those staff, how many days/weeks/months it will take them to complete the activity.

Taking all these factors into account, here is Stella's list of estimated times for activities:

| Key activity | | Estimated time in weeks |
|---|---|---|
| A | Draw up proposals for redesign of reception area and <u>café</u> | 2 |
| B, D, K | Consult with clients | 3 |
| C | Organize redecoration and installation of new furniture | 4 |
| E | Organize deliveries of requested drinks and snacks | 1 |
| F | Establish checking and cleaning procedures | 1 |
| G | Draw up rota for checking and cleaning procedures | 1 |
| H | Establish procedures for maintenance of gym equipment | 1 |
| I | Draw up rota for checking equipment | 1 |
| J | Draw up new list of classes | 1 |
| L | Recruit teachers for classes | 8 |
| M, O | Organize client care session | 1 |
| N | Set up appointments system for gym during peak periods | 1 |
| P | Run client care session | Half-day |
| Q | Establish system for client care in gym | 2 |
| R | Organize and produce publicity brochure | 6 |
| S | Distribute brochure | 2 |

If you now add times to the various activities in the logic diagram, you will see which route from Start to Finish will take the **longest** time. This route is the critical path – the **minimum** amount of time it will take to complete the project.

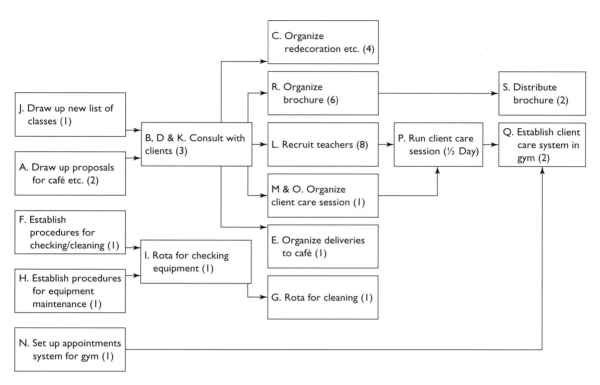

Critical path diagram for health club change project

In Stella's diagram, the critical path is A (2 weeks), K (three weeks), L (eight weeks), P (half a day) and Q (two weeks) – a total of 15 weeks. So if everything goes according to plan, the whole project should take less than four months. In reality, there could be some slippage. It may, for example, take more than eight weeks to recruit all the teachers. However, the diagram does establish the basis for week-by-week planning and monitoring.

# Activity 26

You can practise producing your own logic and critical path diagrams by starting with something simple, such as preparing a meal. Imagine you are asked to prepare the following menu:

- scrubbed and boiled new potatoes;
- cheese omelette;
- salad with dressing;
- strawberries and cream.

Draw a logic diagram and then a critical path diagram with the time for each task in minutes.

The task that is going to take the longest time in this menu is scrubbing and boiling the new potatoes. In fact, it is probable that this task alone will constitute your critical path. Parallel to it will be all the other tasks. All you need to do is work out how long each one is going to take and the best order in which to do them, ending with cooking the omelette.

## 5.3 Gantt charts

A Gantt chart, which is often in the form of a bar chart, shows all the key activities and when they should begin or end. (The activities are listed down the left hand side and the timescale appears across the top.) The chart doesn't, however, show the relationship between different activities as clearly as a critical path diagram.

A Gantt chart for Stella's project would look like the one on page 47.

In this chart, a number of activities are all shown starting in the first week. But in fact, if the main priority is to get all elements of the project completed by the time the publicity brochure is distributed, rather than making lots of small improvements over a period of time, there are a number of activities that could be completed as late as week 13 (Activities F, G, H, I and N). These activities have what is referred to as 'float'. This is shown on the chart by the addition of a line. It's also apparent that organizing the client care session for staff (Activity M) could begin earlier. This activity is therefore said to have 'slack'. It's always useful to have some activities with float or slack as they will give you some flexibility in the schedule, which will probably be much-needed.

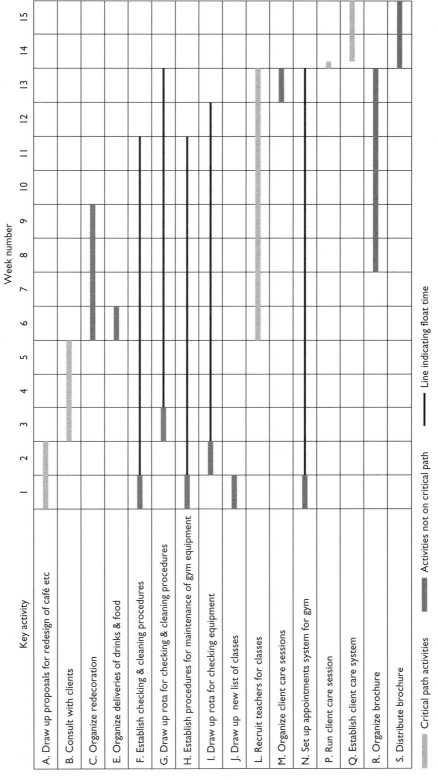

Gantt chart for health club change project

# Activity 27

15 mins

The health club project has several sub-projects, one of which is to produce and distribute a publicity brochure. The critical path analysis for this sub-project looks like this:

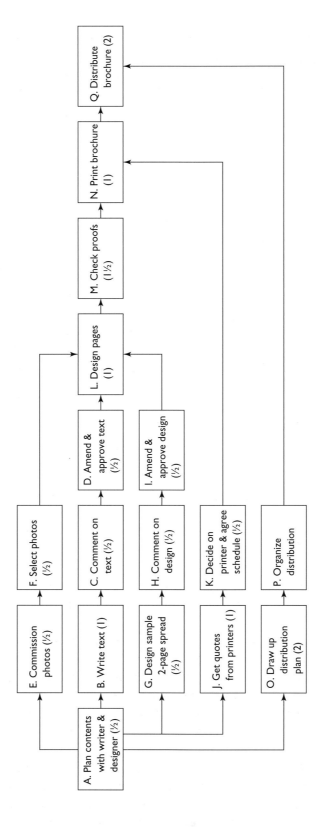

Try producing a Gantt chart for this sub-project using the outline overleaf. (Bear in mind that the printers may need to be informed at least a week before printing that they have been chosen to do the job.)

Week number

| Activity | 1 | 2 | 3 | 4 | 5 | 6 | 7 | 8 |
|---|---|---|---|---|---|---|---|---|
|  |  |  |  |  |  |  |  |  |
|  |  |  |  |  |  |  |  |  |
|  |  |  |  |  |  |  |  |  |
|  |  |  |  |  |  |  |  |  |
|  |  |  |  |  |  |  |  |  |
|  |  |  |  |  |  |  |  |  |
|  |  |  |  |  |  |  |  |  |
|  |  |  |  |  |  |  |  |  |
|  |  |  |  |  |  |  |  |  |
|  |  |  |  |  |  |  |  |  |
|  |  |  |  |  |  |  |  |  |
|  |  |  |  |  |  |  |  |  |
|  |  |  |  |  |  |  |  |  |
|  |  |  |  |  |  |  |  |  |
|  |  |  |  |  |  |  |  |  |
|  |  |  |  |  |  |  |  |  |

You can see a completed Gantt Chart on page 81.

Other information that can be added to a Gantt chart includes:

■ milestones (that is, special points where you think it's important to check on progress so far), perhaps represented by a diamond or triangle
■ project meetings, perhaps represented by a circle.

As you can see, it is a fairly easy task to draw a Gantt chart. However, computer software is available that will enable you to try out a number of different scenarios very quickly, showing what will happen if an activity takes a longer or shorter period of time than you originally forecast. Using the software will also make life much easier when it comes to monitoring the project's progress and making any necessary adjustments from week to week.

When drawing up a project plan, you need to bear in mind that plans have a tendency to go astray. So always aim to build some **contingency time** into your plan – and possibly some **contingency resources** – to help you cope with the unexpected. There are all sorts of ways in which things could go wrong for Stella: a vital staff member could fall ill; there may be a delay in the delivery of the furniture; there may be a problem with getting a piece of equipment fixed, and so on. Rather than telling the club owner that the project will be completed in under four months, she should make it clear that this is the **minimum** amount of time it will take.

# 6 Establishing responsibilities and methods of communication

As well as sorting out the key project activities and overall schedule, you need to establish exactly who is responsible for what. Whether you do this during the stage of planning the activities, or afterwards, will depend on the particular situation. However, whenever you do it, remember that if your team is to feel empowered, every member must have an established responsibility within the project.

Going back to Stella and the health club, for example, she would be making a big mistake if she thought she could manage all the key activities herself. In one of the initial team meetings it needs to be agreed exactly who will take responsibility for organizing the customer survey, who will take responsibility for sorting out the refurbishment of the café and reception area, and so on. In this particular example, the ideal time to do this may have been after the team had drawn up the logic diagram but before they started on the critical path diagram. However, this may not always be the case.

## 6.1 Identifying possible effects

Giving people new responsibilities not only means empowering them; it also means identifying what new skills they need to acquire. If they require further training, this may have the knock-on effect of an additional cost.

You will also need to consider the effects of the change not only on each member of your team, but also on the people outside your team – that is, the 'ripple' effects. It's essential that you discuss your plans for change with these people and together make an assessment of how they will be affected. You may need to consider ways of amending your plan to accommodate the requirements of people outside your team. Going through this process will have the added benefit of helping to break down any existing barriers between departments.

One major question to consider is: who is likely to resist the change, and how will you deal with this resistance? Never ignore signs of resistance or try to overcome it just by repeating arguments in support of change. Instead, as we saw in Session A, attempt to understand the reasons for the resistance and be prepared to discuss these while pointing to the possible benefits of change for the individuals concerned.

## Activity 28

**S/NVQ C6**

This Activity may provide the basis of appropriate evidence for your S/NVQ portfolio. If you are intending to take this course of action, write your answers on separate sheets of paper.

Look back at your notes in Activity 16b on a change project and consider the following questions:

a How will each individual in your team be affected by the change?

_____

_____

b What further training or development activities, if any, do they need to take part in?

_____

_____

c Which other groups (if any) will be affected? How will they be affected?

_____

_____

d What role should you play in dealing with these effects?

_____

_____

e What are the likely effects (if any) on costs of all of the above?

_____

_____

# 6.2 Identifying lines and methods of communication

If the project is to run smoothly, you also need to ensure that there is good communication throughout. This means not only two-way communication between you and your team, but also keeping people outside the project informed about progress.

**Activity 29**

8 mins

**S/NVQ C6**

This Activity may provide the basis of appropriate evidence for your S/NVQ portfolio. If you are intending to take this course of action, write your answers on separate sheets of paper.

Look back at your notes in Activity 16b on a change project and consider the following questions:

a Who are the people who need to be kept informed?

_____

_____

_____

b At what stages in the project should they be informed?

_____

_____

_____

c What are the best ways of informing them?

_____

_____

_____

The people who need to be kept informed will certainly include your manager. They may also include people in other departments or teams in your organization as well as all the members of your own team. The methods you use may include:

- memos and/or emails;
- regular written reports on progress, with reference to milestones;
- informal one-to-one conversations with your manager and team members;

- regular progress meetings with the whole team;
- ad hoc meetings with the team to sort out major problems as they arise.

It's a good idea to include team progress meetings in your schedule. However, never regard these as a substitute for other forms of communication. Rather, always be ready to listen and respond appropriately to the concerns voiced by members of your team and so keep up the team's morale.

We will return to the subject of communication in the next session.

## Self-assessment 2

20 mins

For each of the statements 1 to 4, state whether it is TRUE or FALSE, and write a brief sentence explaining why.

1    Change that crosses departmental boundaries is always
     instigated by senior management.                              TRUE/FALSE

_____

_____

2    It is not enough to just 'sell' an idea for change to your
     staff. You must also empower them to control the
     necessary activities themselves.                              TRUE/FALSE

_____

_____

3    It isn't change that creates anxiety in staff so
     much as uncertainty about change.                             TRUE/FALSE

_____

_____

4    During a change project it is essential not to distract
     staff from the job in hand by constantly providing them
     with information.                                             TRUE/FALSE

_____

_____

For questions 5 to 7, complete the sentences with a suitable word or words from the following list:

SCOPE                    ACTIVITIES              COMMUNICATION
TIMESCALE                RESOURCES               OBJECTIVES

5  The first step in planning a change project is to define the _____ of the project.

6  It's very important to establish the _____ of a project as early as possible so that you know what you are setting out to achieve.

7  Once you have a rough idea of the project's _____ and the available _____, you can begin to plan the _____.

8  Good _____ always helps a project to run smoothly.

For questions 9 to 11, circle the type of diagram that is being described.

9  This is in the form of a bar chart which shows all the key activities and when they should begin or end.

LOGIC DIAGRAM/CRITICAL PATH DIAGRAM/GANTT CHART

10  This helps you to identify the key stages in a project and the order in which they should occur.

LOGIC DIAGRAM/CRITICAL PATH DIAGRAM/GANTT CHART

11  This shows the relationship between different activities, identifying which activities may run in parallel to each other and which must follow on consecutively from each other.

LOGIC DIAGRAM/CRITICAL PATH DIAGRAM/GANTT CHART

12  In a Gantt chart some activities have 'slack', while others have 'float'. Which of the following statements about these terms are correct?

a  An activity is said to have 'float' if its completion date could be earlier than that shown in the chart. CORRECT/NOT CORRECT

b  Float is shown on the chart by the addition of a line. CORRECT/NOT CORRECT

c  An activity is said to have 'slack' if its completion date could be later than that shown in the chart. CORRECT/NOT CORRECT

d  Slack is shown on the chart by the addition of a line. CORRECT/NOT CORRECT

Answers to these questions can be found on 82.

# 7 Summary

- There are many aspects to the role of a first line manager in change. They include:

  - instigating change;
  - calculating costs;
  - determining feasibility;
  - feeding back information to management;
  - keeping the team informed;
  - working out a strategy for deployment of staff;
  - coping with keeping things running during the change.

- It's important for a first line manager to win the support of their team for a proposed change. This means:

  - 'selling' the idea of change to the team;
  - empowering the team to cope with the change;
  - providing the team with the feeling of ownership of the change.

- A major change can be treated as a project or number of projects.

- The first steps in planning a change project are to establish the scope of the change and its aims and objectives.

- The next steps in project planning are to:

  - establish the approximate timescale and financial constraints within which you are working;
  - establish what staff and other resources you will need or are available to you;
  - identify the main project activities.

- Tools to help you in planning how you are going to achieve a project's aims and objectives are:

  - logic diagrams;
  - critical path diagrams;
  - Gantt charts.

- Constructing a logic diagram will help you to identify the key stages in a project and the order in which they should occur.

- A critical path diagram shows the relationship between different activities, identifying which activities may run in parallel to each other and which must follow on consecutively from each other.

- A Gantt chart is a bar chart that shows all the key activities in a project and when they should begin and end. Computer software is available that will not only help you to draw Gantt charts but also try out different scenarios very quickly.

- Once the project activities have been planned, you need to establish responsibilities. You also need to ensure that there will be effective communication both within your team and with people outside it.

# Session C
## Implementing change and managing its consequences

# 1 Introduction

We all know that in real life not everything goes according to plan. This means that when you implement a change project plan, you must be ready to:

- undertake thorough monitoring throughout the project;
- make adjustments to plans.

The good news is that if you have been thorough in your initial planning, this dual task of monitoring and making adjustments will be a lot easier.

However, no amount of planning can make dealing with the mixed emotions that change can arouse in people any easier. There may well be times when you will need all your interpersonal skills to cope with signs of stress among your staff. And you will certainly need not only to maintain your own enthusiasm for change wherever possible, but also to communicate this enthusiasm to others.

Even when a change project comes to an end, your role in managing change is not over. Remember, it's always important to acknowledge what has been achieved and celebrate this with staff – even if it's clear that you will soon be embarking on further change.

# 2 Monitoring the project plan

The first thing to note about monitoring is that it is impossible to carry it out unless you have good communication. It is only through communication that you will learn how the project is progressing and whether adjustments have to be made to the plan to deal with any deviations.

The monitoring process generally consists of the following stages:

- collect information, mainly from team members;
- check progress against plan and identify any deviations;
- identify the cause of any deviations and find solutions;
- when necessary, gain approval for changes in plan;
- implement solutions to bring the project back on track.

## 2.1 Types of deviation from the plan

One of the most common types of deviation you can expect to find is the amount of time spent on an activity. At the beginning of a project it's very easy to be over-optimistic about how much can be achieved in a particular amount of time. Of course, sometimes you are set an ultimate deadline and have no choice but to try and achieve it – even when you know it's going to be very difficult to do so. On the other hand, the amount of time allotted to activities in the planning of a project may not be unduly optimistic, and the only reason that an activity is not completed when it's supposed to be is poor time management.

One way of dealing with slippages in the schedule can be to employ more resources, whether they be in the form of people, equipment or materials. However, a lack of resources may in itself be a cause of deviation. Suddenly finding yourself without vital staff for whatever reason can throw the best-laid plan into confusion, and some people with particular skills are very difficult to replace at short notice.

Imagine, for example, a pub that is relying on an excellent, recently employed, chef to help restore the reputation of its restaurant and so build up its customer base. The owner has initiated a small change project with the aim of reaching a certain weekly profit. If the chef suddenly has to take time off work, what can the pub owner do when the agency chef sent to replace him turns out to be bad at his job? He may decide that it's actually better to close the restaurant for a few days, and delay achieving his goal, rather than jeopardize the whole project by serving customers with low-quality meals.

This brings us to something else that can go wrong with projects: the quality of the outcomes at certain stages. It may sometimes be necessary, as a last resort, to accept a reduction in the quality of an activity's outcome if this is the only way to get the project back on track. Suppose, for example, that part of the pub owner's change project is to improve the garden. He may have imagined a wonderful display of flowers and then found that certain plants fail to flourish because of the poor soil. In such a situation the best strategy is to revise his plans for the garden!

In short, you'll find that deviation from a project plan occurs most often in:

- the time spent on activities;
- the resources used;
- the quality of activity outcomes.

## Activity 30

**S/NVQ C6**

This Activity may provide the basis of appropriate evidence for your S/NVQ portfolio. If you are intending to take this course of action, it might be better to write your answers on separate sheets of paper.

Look back at the notes you wrote in Activity 16a regarding a change project in which you and your team have been involved.

- What deviations from the plan occurred?

_____

_____

- What measures did you or anybody else take to put the plan back on track?

_____

_____

## 2.2 Tracking progress

Keeping track of where you are in your plan is a lot easier if you have produced a critical path diagram and Gantt chart. This is particularly so if you have used computer software to produce your Gantt chart. You can then make any necessary adjustments to your chart as you go along and leave the software to reveal what the possible knock-on effects might be. To see how helpful a Gantt chart can be, let's return to the publicity brochure for the health club.

> At the beginning of week 5 of the project, Stella begins to organize the new publicity brochure. She has already warned the copy-writer and designer who normally work on the club's promotional literature that a new brochure is required, so she doesn't expect any problems in the early stages. However, when she rings up the copy-writer to ask him to come in for a meeting she discovers that he is in the middle of desperately trying to meet a deadline for another project and would like to delay their meeting for a week. Stella feels she has no alternative but to agree.
>
> Stella next rings the designer to arrange for her to come to the same meeting as the copy-writer. This is no problem. However, when the meeting takes place, Stella discovers that the designer is due to go on holiday for a week in three weeks' time. Will this mean that the brochure will end up delaying the 'Finish' date of the whole project? Looking at the Gantt chart and making a couple of adjustments will give her the answer.

## Activity 31

*5 mins*

Have a look at the Gantt chart you produced for Activity 27. If you make the adjustments that allow for the delayed meeting with the copy-writer and for the designer's holiday, what will the knock-on effects be?

■ When will the brochure be ready to go to the printer?

_____

■ Will the brochure be distributed before the agreed project 'Finish' date? If not, how late will it be?

_____

Delaying the initial meeting with the copy-writer by one week – so that it takes place in week 7 rather than week 6 – adds a week to the schedule. The designer's holiday in week 10 adds another week. This means the brochure will go to the printer in week 12 rather than week 10. This is fine, as the brochure is not due to be distributed until week 14. However, if there is any further slippage, the project will not be completed on time. It will become necessary for Stella to make some additional plans, such as getting either the copy-writer or designer to work late in the evening or at the weekend.

## 2.3  Identifying problems

In monitoring a project it's always helpful to have some idea about the types of problem that might arise. They could be to do with:

- staff – key people not being there when needed because of, for example, illness;
- physical resources – buildings, equipment or materials being defective in some way;
- technology – systems not working as they are supposed to;
- finance – promised money not being available after all, or various activities within the project going over budget;
- procedures – a process not going as expected.

Whatever the nature of the problem, you may have to undertake some serious problem solving with your team. This could entail:

- collecting whatever information is necessary to define the problem correctly;
- identifying possible causes;
- identifying possible solutions;
- choosing the best solution;
- implementing and evaluating the solution.

Another workbook in this series, *Solving Problems and Making Decisions*, gives far more detail than we've got space for here. Suffice it to say here that among the tools you can use to help analyse the causes of problems is the **fishbone** or **cause and effect diagram.**

If you look at a critical path diagram for a project, you may well be able to identify various points at which problems are particularly likely to arise.

## Activity 32 · 3 mins

Take another look at the critical path diagram for the health club project on page 45. If you were Stella, what are the points at which you would want to keep a particularly close watch for problems?

_____

_____

There are a number of possible answers to this question. However, it's fair to say that one obvious point at which there could be problems is after the consultation with clients. As a general rule, activities that follow a merge need to be watched closely, as do activities that:

■ are expected to take a long time to complete (such as the recruitment of teachers for the health club);

■ have little or no float or slack (such as the drawing up of proposals for the café and reception area);

■ involve a lot of people (such as establishing a client care system in the gym);

■ involve new technology (as the appointments and client care systems might do if it was decided to computerize them);

■ require people to do something they haven't done before (again, as in establishing a client care system in the gym).

## 2.4 Evaluating the project

Going hand in hand with the monitoring of a project is evaluation. While monitoring is about comparing what actually happened with what was planned, evaluation goes one step further and involves drawing conclusions about:

■ what has been achieved;

■ what has gone well or badly;

■ why things have gone the way they have;

■ what can be done better next time.

Evaluation does not all have to be done at the end of a project. In fact, it is best done at pre-defined points in a project's life. Lessons can then be learned and acted upon as the project progresses.

# Activity 33

Imagine you are in Stella's position at the health club. You decide that a good point at which to evaluate what has happened so far is after two subgroups of three people have drawn up the proposals for the café and reception area, and produced a list of classes. What could you hope to learn from the evaluation that you might feed back into the subsequent stages of the project?

_____

_____

_____

One of the basic things you might hope to learn is how efficient each of the subgroups is in meeting a deadline for completing a task such as drawing up proposals. After talking to members of the two groups, you might also discover who is more likely to act as a leader, who has good organizing talents, who is particularly committed to establishing a broad range of classes, and so on. This information can then be used to ensure that the most suitable people take on basic organizational tasks, such as setting up rotas, while the person particularly committed to expanding the classes becomes the one responsible for recruiting teachers.

# 3 Completing a change project

How do you know when a change project is completed? One obvious answer might be: 'When the final activity in the project plan has been completed' Another might be: 'When all the objectives have been met'. However, in reality, the original objectives and planned activities may have to be amended as the project evolves and as factors arise that are outside the control of you and your team – such as developments in the external environment. Furthermore, even the achievement of SMART objectives is not always possible to assess straight away. Suppose, for example, that one of the objectives of the health club project is that 'All clients in the gym should have their exercise needs assessed on a weekly basis'. It will take a few weeks for this to be put into practice and for data to be collected on whether, in fact, clients' needs are being properly assessed. And then various steps might have to be taken to improve the assessment of needs.

In fact, in the majority of change projects it's best never to think of them as ever totally completed. (There are notable exceptions to this rule – as when the change is a change of premises.) Generally speaking, there is always room for improvement. Once the final activity in a project plan has been carried out, the best course is to keep on monitoring the outcomes and collect feedback that can be used as the basis for a programme of continual improvement.

At the same time you need to find a way of acknowledging your team's achievements in a change project and joining your team in some form of celebration. Different teams celebrate in different ways. Some take a night out together; others are happy to be allowed time for 'pet' projects. You could send a letter of thanks, addressed either to the team as a whole, or to each person individually. It is very important to show appreciation for an endeavour above and beyond the call of normal duty.

# Activity 34 · 5 mins

S/NVQ
C6

This Activity may provide the basis of appropriate evidence for your S/NVQ portfolio. If you are intending to take this course of action, it might be better to write your answers on separate sheets of paper.

Look back at the notes you wrote in Activity 16a regarding a change project in which you and your team have been involved.

■ At what point, if any, did you or your manager acknowledge that the project's main aims had been achieved?

_____

■ Having made this acknowledgment, were there any follow-on activities aimed at achieving further improvement? If so, what were they? If not, are there any follow-on activities that you think should have taken place?

_____

_____

## 3.1 Change fatigue

As well as acknowledging people's achievements, you also need to recognize that after a period of sustained effort, people often feel flat and tired. The completion of the final activity in the project plan may come as something of an anticlimax. Time is needed to recover: nobody can work at an intense level for long without a period of recuperation.

Unfortunately, this is not always recognized, with the result that in some workplaces people suffer from what is known as 'change fatigue'. They begin to feel that change is being instigated for its own sake, and without any apparent overall plan. As change after change takes place, they naturally become reluctant to co-operate, wondering when the latest project will be supplanted by another one.

# Activity 35

Have you ever suffered from change fatigue? Apart from stopping the programme of change, was there any particular action by management that may have helped to alleviate it?

_____

_____

_____

Your answer to the question in Activity 35 will depend on your particular circumstances. However, there is one general rule that all managers at all levels can follow where there is a danger of change fatigue: keep staff informed about why change is necessary from the earliest possible date.

# 3.2 Life after redundancies

A theme throughout this workbook has been that change is necessary and has many benefits for both organizations and individual staff alike. However, there are some types of change in organizations that can have adverse effects on people, the most obvious of which is redundancy.

We hear a lot about the trauma suffered by people who have been made redundant. This is understandable. Security of employment hardly exists any more, and we are naturally sympathetic when someone suddenly finds himself or herself without a job. To go through a career without having been made redundant seems to be an exceptional feat these days.

Another problem that is very real, but which is given far less publicity, is that of the employees left behind after a 'pruning down' of staff numbers. The survivors of redundancy often feel threatened, guilty and overworked, and they need special handling.

If you have ever found yourself in the position of managing a team following a spate of redundancies, you will know the importance of:

- building team cohesion and morale back up;
- returning work routines to normal as soon as possible;
- watching out for signs of stress;
- pacing the workload, so that the new team can quickly recover their sense of pride and achievement, and not become overwhelmed by the backlog piling up.

In the period immediately following the redundancies, it may be good policy to step up the rate of work, to get over the 'change crisis'. You may find that the team members feel they need to do more to help them get over their sense of guilt. However, it is usually a mistake to make that the norm.

Redundancies are often caused by restructuring programmes. Such programmes can give new responsibilities to the remaining staff – responsibilities that they do not always feel equipped to handle. One response to this situation can be to feel inadequate and stressed; another can be to see it as a welcome opportunity to develop new skills. This can apply as much to first line managers as it does to team members.

## Activity 36 · 5 mins

Have you ever been in a situation where a change programme required you to develop new skills? If you haven't, try to think of someone you know who has. What was your/their response?

_____

_____

_____

_____

What help were you given in developing these skills?

_____

_____

_____

_____

What did you/they learn from this experience about how to regard change in the future?

_____

_____

_____

_____

EXTENSIONS 2 and 3
An overview of what's involved in managing change is supplied by Extension 2, *Managing Change* by Robert Heller. You will find more detailed accounts in Extension 3, *Harvard Business Review on Change*.

You may have had a negative experience, but hopefully you have learned that change is not something to avoid whenever possible. Rather, it has the potential to provide exciting new opportunities to develop the skills of both you and your staff and help your organization to prosper in a constantly changing environment.

## Self-assessment 3 · 10 mins

1   Complete the following steps in the monitoring process with a suitable word chosen from the following list.

PLAN               INFORMATION        SOLUTIONS
DEVIATIONS         CHANGES            CAUSE

■ Collect _____, mainly from team members
■ Check progress against _____ and identify any _____
■ Identify the _____ of any deviations and find solutions
■ When necessary, gain approval for _____ in plan
■ Implement _____ to bring the project back on track

2   The main types of problems that can arise during the implementation of projects are to do with staff, physical resources, technology, finance and procedures. Can you say a bit more about what these problems are likely to be?

■ Staff

_____

_____

■ Physical resources

_____

_____

■ Technology

_____

_____

■ Finance

_____

_____

■ Procedures

_____

_____

3    What process is described by each of the following?

a It consists of drawing conclusions about what has been achieved, why things have gone the way they have, and what can be done better next time.

_____

b It consists of identifying the reasons why something has gone wrong, and identifying and implementing a solution.

_____

c It consists of comparing what has actually happened with what was planned and responding accordingly.

_____

4    Which of the following statements are good advice to the leader of a team that has just participated in a major change? What is wrong with the statements that you think are not good advice?

a Always make a point of acknowledging what has been achieved.

b Avoid celebrating the end of a change project when another change project is imminent.

c Recognize that people may feel flat and tired after a project and give them time to recuperate.

d If staff are suffering from change fatigue, cut down on the amount of information you give them about the next change project.

e If the change has involved redundancies, bear in mind that the survivors may feel threatened and guilty.

f Immediately after redundancies have been made, never increase the workload of the survivors.

_____

_____

_____

_____

_____

Answers to these questions can be found on page 83.

# 4 Summary

- Good communication is the key to monitoring change successfully.

- The most common forms of deviation from a plan for change are in:
  - the time spent on individual activities;
  - the resources used;
  - the quality of activity outcomes.

- Keeping track of progress is made a lot easier by the use of a critical path diagram and Gantt chart.

- Problems that arise during a change project may be to do with:
  - staff;
  - physical resources;
  - technology;
  - finance;
  - procedures.

- Going hand in hand with monitoring is evaluation, which involves drawing conclusions about:
  - what has been achieved;
  - what has gone well or badly;
  - why things have gone the way they have;
  - what can be done better next time.

- It's always important to mark the end of a change project in some way and, whenever possible, celebrate what has been achieved.

- Too much change can result in 'change fatigue'. People need time to recover after a major change project.

- Change involving redundancies can have an adverse effect on the survivors as well as on those made redundant. In such situations you will need to pay close attention to building up morale and pacing the workload.

- Change has the potential to provide exciting new opportunities for both you and your staff to develop new skills.

# Performance checks

## 1 Quick quiz

Jot down the answers to the following questions on *Understanding Change in the Workplace*.

Question 1   What do you identify when you carry out a force field analysis?

_____

_____

Question 2   What do the letters PIE stand for in the 'recipe' for overcoming resistance to change?

_____

Question 3   What is meant by 'unfreezing' and 'refreezing' in connection with change?

_____

_____

_____

Question 4   As a team leader, what are two of the suitable courses of action for you in the refreezing stage?

_____

_____

_____

Question 5   In planning a change project you begin by defining the project's scope, aims and objectives. Is there anything else you need to establish before doing any detailed planning of the project activities?

_____

_____

Question 6     What does a critical path diagram show about the key activities in a project? What does a Gantt chart show?

_____

_____

_____

Question 7     What is the one thing that is essential to the successful monitoring of a plan?

_____

Question 8     Name one of the most common forms of deviation from a project plan.

_____

Question 9     What is the main difference between monitoring and evaluation?

_____

_____

_____

Answers to these questions can be found on page 84.

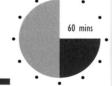

# 2 Workbook assessment

Imagine you work for a small organization (with anything between 20 and 50 employees) and you have been asked by your manager to attend a meeting at which ideas are to be discussed on how to attract – and keep – more customers for the organization's product or service.

Some weeks after this meeting, your manager tells you that the organization has decided to make a number of important changes, one of which will mean some restructuring. There will be no redundancies, but people will be moved into different departments and will have to acquire some new skills. You will end up with a department consisting of two of your present staff and two new staff.

Consider the following questions.

- What difficulties are there likely to be?
- How will you go about preparing your staff for the change?
- How will you help your staff through the actual change?

- How will you try to deal with any worries or problems among your staff after the change?
- How will you plan for the change?
- What planning tool could you use to help you implement the change programme?

Write a paragraph on each of these questions.

Make any assumptions you wish about the kind of work that the company does. If you wish, you can base any details not defined above on your own job, or one that you have done in the past.

Your complete answer to this assessment need not be longer than a single page.

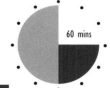

# 3 Work-based assignment

**S/NVQ
C6**

The time guide for this assignment gives you an approximate idea of how long it is likely to take you to write up your findings. You will find you need to spend some additional time gathering information, talking to colleagues and thinking about the assignment. The results of your efforts should be presented on separate sheets of paper.

The assignment may provide the basis of appropriate evidence for your S/NVQ portfolio.

**What you have
to do**

For this assignment, identify a fairly major change that you expect to happen in the near future. If you wish, return to the change that you first identified in Activity 16b (and subsequently considered in Activities 21, 23, 24, 28 and 29).

Write a few sentences defining the scope of the project (and the date by which it is to be completed if this is known). Then, consulting with members of your team wherever possible, carry out the following:

- Draw up a list of aims and objectives for your team in implementing the change. Wherever possible, make the objectives:

    - specific;
    - measurable;
    - achievable;
    - relevant;
    - timebound.

(Bear in mind that it may not always be possible to produce SMART objectives until you have done more detailed planning. However, you should be able to identify the main aims of the project.)

■ Draw up a list of the main activities that your team must undertake in order to achieve the objectives. (Aim to keep this list as short as possible – a maximum of 12 activities would be ideal for this assignment.)

■ Establish what resources you need to complete these activities in terms of:

— staff (including hours, abilities and skills);
— other resources (such as equipment);
— approximate budget.

■ Establish whether any of your team members will require additional training or development to acquire the necessary skills.

**What you should write**

■ Write a concise project outline that contains the following information:

— the project's scope;
— aims and objectives;
— timescale (which may only be approximate at this initial stage);
— necessary resources, including staff time, abilities and skills;
— any necessary additional training or development for staff;
— budget (which again may only be approximate at this initial stage).

■ Draw the following diagrams to help you plan the project:

— a logic diagram (which begins with 'Start' and ends with 'Finish' but has no timescale and focuses on showing which activities are dependent on other activities);
— a critical path diagram (which shows how long individual activities will take and the chain of activities that will take the longest time between 'Start' and 'Finish');
— a Gantt chart (showing the activities and timescale, plus possible milestones where you think it will be important to check on progress to date).

■ Once you have completed your diagrams, write a concise paragraph explaining how you might use them in implementing and monitoring the change project.

■ Finally, write a brief paragraph on communication throughout the project, stating whom you will need to keep informed on progress and problems, and the methods you will use for doing this.

The written part of this document does not have to be more than two or three pages long. You will probably need a separate sheet of paper for each diagram.

# Reflect and review

##  1 Reflect and review

Now that you have completed your work on *Understanding Change in the Workplace*, let's review our workbook objectives. First:

- You should be better able to anticipate and recognize reactions to a proposed change, and overcome resistance to the change.

Reactions, as we have seen, will depend very much on:

- the way that a change is presented;
- how well the team leader or manager is able to 'sell' the idea of the change;
- how much thought is given to the way in which information is released.

No matter how you present a change, you have to be prepared for at least some resistance to it. In the initial stages of a change project you need to consider the exact nature of this resistance and what you can do to reduce it – two-way communication will play a key role here. Once the change is underway, you can smooth its progress by ensuring that:

- the team has the opportunity to participate in the planning process;
- team members are given the information, knowledge and skills they need to handle the change;
- you demonstrate enthusiasm – bearing in mind that in some situations this just isn't possible.

You might like to ask the following questions.

- What can I do to improve my ability to recognize and anticipate reactions among my team?

_____

_____

_____

■ What more can I do to ensure that my team have sufficient opportunity to participate in planning a change?

_____

_____

_____

■ What more can I do to ensure that my team are always given the information, knowledge and skills they need to handle a particular change?

_____

_____

_____

The second workbook objective was:

■ You will be better able to plan change projects.

A huge amount of work can go into planning major change. In fact, in some cases it's better to think of a major change as a number of projects rather than one. Whatever the size of the project, there are always certain processes that you will need to go through, such as:

■ collecting information;
■ establishing the aims and objectives;
■ establishing the timescale and necessary resources (including budget and staff);
■ assessing the feasibility of the project;
■ identifying the necessary activities and planning the order in which they are to be done, and by whom.

There are various tools you can use in planning projects, such as critical path diagrams and Gantt charts. For larger projects you will find them indispensable.

Two questions you may like to ask yourself are:

■ To what extent have I properly planned change in the past? What are the main areas in which I have not been sufficiently thorough in my planning?

_____

_____

_____

■ How might I improve my project-planning skills, including the use of critical path diagrams and Gantt charts?

_____

_____

_____

The next workbook objective was:

■ You will be better able to manage the implementation of change.

Fundamental to managing the implementation of change is communication. Before a change project gets underway you need to consider whom you must keep informed about progress and problems, and how you are going to do this. You also need to identify who is likely to be affected by the change, both within and outside your team, and have a strategy for dealing with any adverse effects and the resistance you may encounter.

Finally, remember that the more thoroughly you plan the change, the easier you will find it to implement. Being able regularly to compare progress with what has been planned, using such tools as Gantt charts, will alert you to problems as they arise and enable you to deal with them before their knock-on effects become too serious.

Questions you might find it useful to consider are:

■ In past change projects, have I paid sufficient attention to communication, both within and outside my team? What might I have done to improve the amount and form of communication?

_____

_____

_____

■ What are the types of problems that have arisen in past change projects? Did I have sufficient skills to deal with them? If not, in what ways do I need to develop my skills?

_____

_____

_____

Our final objective was:

■ You will be better able to monitor and evaluate change projects.

Remember that monitoring is an ongoing process that not only enables you to keep track of progress but also to adjust your plans to take account of unforeseen problems and delays. It is important to make sure that communications are good within the project team, so that problems may be picked up informally, but also to establish regular monitoring points so that any problems that have not been noticed already will be picked up. Monitoring is also a process from which you can learn, as is evaluation, which is basically concerned with drawing conclusions about what has/has not been achieved and why things have gone the way they have.

Questions you might like to consider in relation to monitoring and evaluation are:

■ Have I monitored change projects sufficiently in the past? What sort of problems did monitoring alert me to? Were there other problems of which I was not aware at the time because of insufficient monitoring?

_____

_____

_____

■ If I have evaluated projects, has this only happened at the end or at various points in the project's life? What have I learnt from the evaluation process that I was able to apply to future projects?

_____

_____

_____

# 2 Action plan

Use this plan to further develop for yourself a course of action you want to take. Make a note in the left-hand column of the issues or problems you want to tackle, and then decide what you want to do, and make a note in column 2.

The resources you need might include time, materials, information or money. You may need to negotiate for some of them, but they could be something easily acquired, like half an hour of somebody's time, or a chapter of a book. Put whatever you need in column 3. No plan means anything without a timescale, so put a realistic target completion date in column 4.

Finally, describe the outcome you want to achieve as a result of this plan, whether it is for your own benefit or advancement, or a more efficient way of doing things.

| Desired outcomes | | | | |
|---|---|---|---|---|
| 1 Issues | 2 Action | 3 Resources | 4 Target completion | |
| | | | | |
| Actual outcomes | | | | |

# 3 Extensions

**Extension 1**

| | |
|---|---|
| Book | *Handbook for Creative Team Leaders* |
| Author | Tudor Rickards and Susan Moger |
| Edition | 1999 |
| Publisher | Gower |

This book serves as a useful guide to leading teams through the process of creative improvement and change.

**Extension 2**

| | |
|---|---|
| Book | *Essential Managers 12: Managing Change* |
| Author | Robert Heller |
| Edition | 1998 |
| Publisher | Dorling Kindersley |

An easy-to-read overview of the many aspects of change in organizations is provided by this book.

**Extension 3**

| | |
|---|---|
| Book | *Harvard Business Review on Change* |
| Author | Harvard Business Review |
| Edition | 1998 |
| Publisher | Harvard Business School Press |

More in-depth coverage of change management is provided by the HBR articles included in this book. Among the authors is Philip Kotler, the top marketing professor.

These extensions can be taken up via your ILM Centre. They will either have them or will arrange for you to have access to them. However, it may be more convenient to check out the materials with your human resources people at work – they may well give you access. There are other good reasons for approaching your own people, for example they will become aware of your interest and you can involve them in your development.

# 4 Answers to activities

**Answer to Activity 27 on page 48.**

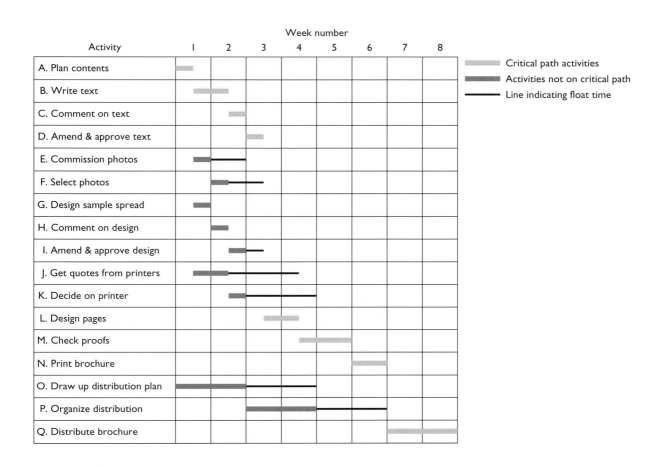

| Activity | Week number | | | | | | | |
|---|---|---|---|---|---|---|---|---|
| | 1 | 2 | 3 | 4 | 5 | 6 | 7 | 8 |
| A. Plan contents | | | | | | | | |
| B. Write text | | | | | | | | |
| C. Comment on text | | | | | | | | |
| D. Amend & approve text | | | | | | | | |
| E. Commission photos | | | | | | | | |
| F. Select photos | | | | | | | | |
| G. Design sample spread | | | | | | | | |
| H. Comment on design | | | | | | | | |
| I. Amend & approve design | | | | | | | | |
| J. Get quotes from printers | | | | | | | | |
| K. Decide on printer | | | | | | | | |
| L. Design pages | | | | | | | | |
| M. Check proofs | | | | | | | | |
| N. Print brochure | | | | | | | | |
| O. Draw up distribution plan | | | | | | | | |
| P. Organize distribution | | | | | | | | |
| Q. Distribute brochure | | | | | | | | |

Critical path activities
Activities not on critical path
Line indicating float time

# 5 Answers to self-assessment questions

**Self-assessment 1 on page 20**

1  a  Resistance to change is NORMAL.
   b  People often resist change because of GENERAL UNCERTAINTY.
   c  As a manager you should focus on how to respond to proposals for change in a CONSTRUCTIVE way.

2  Among the main underlying causes of people's resistance to change is that they see it as a threat to their position, prospects and **prosperity**.

3   You should aim to do both the following when faced with forces opposed to change.

- Maintain the supporting forces at their present level.
- Reduce the opposing forces.

4   a   Where change is concerned, **participation** is the best antidote to resistance.
b   **Information** is the best medicine for uncertainty.
c   **Enthusiasm** is infectious.

**Self-assessment 2 on pages 53–4**

1   It is FALSE that change that crosses departmental boundaries is always insti-gated by senior management.

Change that crosses departmental boundaries can be instigated by any member of staff who keeps an eye open for opportunities for improvement of processes. Some improvements can have knock-on effects throughout an organization.

2   It is TRUE that it's not enough to just 'sell' an idea for change to your staff. You must also empower them to control the necessary activities them-selves. Staff will only become fully committed to change if they feel they have some control over what happens and are not just puppets in the hands of people who have planned a change.

3   It is TRUE that it isn't change that creates anxiety in staff so much as uncer-tainty about change.

It is vital to keep staff well informed about any change programme as soon as you know the broad outline – that is, the scope – of what it will entail.

4   It is FALSE that during a change project it is essential not to distract staff from the job in hand by constantly providing them with information.

Providing staff with information throughout a project has a vital role to play in maintaining commitment and so contributes to the project's success.

5   The first step in planning a change project is to define the **SCOPE** of the project.

6   It's very important to establish the **OBJECTIVES** of a project as early as possible so that you know what you are setting out to achieve.

7   Once you have a rough idea of the project's **TIMESCALE** and the available **RESOURCES**, you can begin to plan the **ACTIVITIES**.

8   Good **COMMUNICATION** always helping a project to run smoothly.

9   A **GANTT CHART** is in the form of a bar chart which shows all the key activities and when they should begin or end.

10   A **LOGIC DIAGRAM** helps you to identify the key stages in a project and the order in which they should occur.

11 A **CRITICAL PATH DIAGRAM** shows the relationship between different activities, identifying which activities may run in parallel to each other and which must follow on consecutively from each other.

12 a It is NOT CORRECT that an activity is said to have 'float' if its completion date could be earlier than that shown in the chart. An activity is said to have float if its completion date could be later.

b It is CORRECT that float is shown on the chart by the addition of a line. The line extends to the latest possible completion date.

c It is NOT CORRECT that an activity is said to have 'slack' if its completion date could be later than that shown in the chart. A statement has slack if it could begin earlier.

d It is NOT CORRECT that slack is shown on the chart by the addition of a line. It is float that is shown by a line.

**Self assessment 3 on pages 67–8**

1 The steps in the monitoring process are as follows:

- Collect **INFORMATION**, mainly from team members
- Check progress against **PLAN** and identify any **DEVIATIONS**
- **Identify the CAUSE** of any deviations and find solutions
- When necessary, gain approval for **CHANGES** in plan
- Implement **SOLUTIONS** to bring the project back on track.

2 **Staff problems** include key people not being there when needed because of, for example, illness.

**Physical resources problems** may be to do with buildings, equipment or materials being defective in some way.

**Technology problems** are often about systems not working as they should.

**Finance problems** can include promised money not being available after all, or various activities within the project going over-budget.

**Procedures problems** are to do with processes not going as expected.

3 a evaluation.
b problem-solving.
c monitoring.

4 b, d and f are not good advice.

b is not good advice because it is always essential to celebrate the end of a project in whatever way is appropriate for the team or situation.

d is not good advice because not providing sufficient information about a change project will only make people feel less empowered, and consequently even less committed than they might otherwise have been to further change.

f is not good advice because sometimes stepping up the rate of work immediately after redundancies can help the survivors to get over their sense of guilt. However, this does **not** mean that the increased rate of work should become the norm.

# 6 Answers to the quick quiz

Answer 1    In carrying out a force field analysis you identify the forces supporting change and the forces opposing change.

Answer 2    The letters PIE in the 'recipe' for overcoming resistance to change stand for participation, information and enthusiasm.

Answer 3    'Unfreezing' means reducing resistance towards change. 'Refreezing' is a word for the process whereby people become familiar with new ideas and new ways, and feel confident about them.

Answer 4    Among the suitable courses of action for you, as a team leader, in the refreezing stage are to:

- be receptive to feedback;
- be prepared to make adjustments to the original plan for change;
- seek the opinions of the workteam.

Answer 5    After defining a project's scope, aims and objectives, you need to establish what the timescale and budget will be, at least approximately.

Answer 6    A critical path diagram shows how the key project activities link to each other, highlighting the chain of activities – the critical path – which determines when the project begins and ends. A Gantt chart shows all the key activities and when they should begin or end. It doesn't, however, show the relationship between different activities as clearly as a critical path diagram.

Answer 7    The one thing that is essential to the successful monitoring of a plan is communication.

Answer 8    The most common forms of deviation from a project plan are:

- the time spent on activities;
- the resources used;
- the quality of activity outcomes.

Answer 9    Monitoring is essentially about comparing what actually happened with what was planned, while evaluation involves drawing conclusions about what has been achieved, why things have gone the way they have, and what can be done better next time.

# 7 Certificate

Completion of the certificate by an authorized person shows that you have worked through all the parts of this workbook and satisfactorily completed the assessments. The certificate provides a record of what you have done that may be used for exemptions or as evidence of prior learning against other nationally certificated qualifications.

# superseries

## Understanding Change
## in the Workplace

..............................................................................

has satisfactorily completed this workbook

Name of signatory   ...................................................................

Position   ...................................................................

Signature   ...................................................................

Date   ...................................................................

Official stamp

**Pergamon**
*Flexible*
**Learning**

Fifth Edition

# **super**series

## FIFTH EDITION

Workbooks in the series:

| | |
|---|---|
| Achieving Objectives Through Time Management | 978-0-08-046415-2 |
| Building the Team | 978-0-08-046412-1 |
| Coaching and Training your Work Team | 978-0-08-046418-3 |
| Communicating One-to-One at Work | 978-0-08-046438-1 |
| Developing Yourself and Others | 978-0-08-046414-5 |
| Effective Meetings for Managers | 978-0-08-046439-8 |
| Giving Briefings and Making Presentations in the Workplace | 978-0-08-046436-7 |
| Influencing Others at Work | 978-0-08-046435-0 |
| Introduction to Leadership | 978-0-08-046411-4 |
| Managing Conflict in the Workplace | 978-0-08-046416-9 |
| Managing Creativity and Innovation in the Workplace | 978-0-08-046441-1 |
| Managing Customer Service | 978-0-08-046419-0 |
| Managing Health and Safety at Work | 978-0-08-046426-8 |
| Managing Performance | 978-0-08-046429-9 |
| Managing Projects | 978-0-08-046425-1 |
| Managing Stress in the Workplace | 978-0-08-046417-6 |
| Managing the Effective Use of Equipment | 978-0-08-046432-9 |
| Managing the Efficient Use of Materials | 978-0-08-046431-2 |
| Managing the Employment Relationship | 978-0-08-046443-5 |
| Marketing for Managers | 978-0-08-046974-4 |
| Motivating to Perform in the Workplace | 978-0-08-046413-8 |
| Obtaining Information for Effective Management | 978-0-08-046434-3 |
| Organizing and Delegating | 978-0-08-046422-0 |
| Planning Change in the Workplace | 978-0-08-046444-2 |
| Planning to Work Efficiently | 978-0-08-046421-3 |
| Providing Quality to Customers | 978-0-08-046420-6 |
| Recruiting, Selecting and Inducting New Staff in the Workplace | 978-0-08-046442-8 |
| Solving Problems and Making Decisions | 978-0-08-046423-7 |
| Understanding Change in the Workplace | 978-0-08-046424-4 |
| Understanding Culture and Ethics in Organizations | 978-0-08-046428-2 |
| Understanding Organizations in their Context | 978-0-08-046427-5 |
| Understanding the Communication Process in the Workplace | 978-0-08-046433-6 |
| Understanding Workplace Information Systems | 978-0-08-046440-4 |
| Working with Costs and Budgets | 978-0-08-046430-5 |
| Writing for Business | 978-0-08-046437-4 |

For prices and availability please telephone our order helpline
or email

+44 (0) 1865 474010
directorders@elsevier.com